I AM THRIVING NOW

From a Life of Emotional Pain to a Beautiful Life of Freedom

11 Steps to Mental Resilience and Self-Love

Peggy Bareh

Dear reader, Jaqui
I hope this book
creates a difference in
your life.
Thanks for your
support.

Book design by Publishing Push

ISBN's
Paperback: 978-1-80227-035-8
eBook: 978-1-80227-036-5

Dedicated to my Grandma
Ma Susan Changsen
who stood by me to give me
a purpose in life, and, to victims
and survivors of abuse and
modern slavery

Table of Contents

Preface

Synopsis

Through my experiences and testimonies of others whose lives have been rocked by emotional or physical trauma, I passionately believe that no one was born to live and die in agony. After being subjected to trauma from childhood, teenage and adulthood abuse, and failures in my life, I felt the need to embark on a journey that could uncover the treasure of my pain. I realised that victims of psychological and physical pain, especially victims of childhood and domestic abuse, are settling for less in life. We are settling for less and not reaching our highest potentials because our dreams and talents in life are held hostage by the devastating impacts of Pain.

From childhood, our experiences damage our mental health. They take away our self-esteem, identity, value, confidence, motivation, passion, happiness, and purpose. This leaves us with anxiety, depression, emptiness, loneliness, confusion, shame, resentment, worthlessness, and hopelessness. It paralyses us with fear to speak, fear to find our identity, fear to escape our worries and pursue our dreams.

Knowing that everyone was born to live a thriving life, I, therefore, needed to find a unique formula for a sustainable recovery – a blueprint for unleashing my happiness. To have a fulfilled life, I needed to Turn my Pain into Gain, if not for my sake but for the sake of my kids. And how could I do that?

For a long time, I grappled with finding the answer to my question - How can I turn my Pain into Gain? Through research, training, and my personal journey, I uncovered the answer in 14 principles which has transformed my life. I AM THRIVING NOW contains 14 letters, with each representing a step to unlocking the treasure of your pain. The first 11 steps are the core steps, and the last three are the bonus, but very vital steps. To write this book, I built on my skills as a Health and Social Care worker and my experience in supporting victims of abuse. And I do so with the hope of unlocking your passion and potential, which becomes an anchor to living a thriving life. I believe that this book will help to walk you through step by step to regain your happiness.

www.iamthrivingnow.com

Disclaimer

I DO NOT write as a philosopher or a professional therapist, but as a victim-author who shares your pain. And I hope that my experiences and findings will inspire you to Turn Your Pain into Gain. Some names and details in this book have been changed to protect identities.

Author's Note

Thank You for Purchasing and Reading this book to the end. Your life won't be the same again!

Who Is This Book For?

This book is for anyone who is broken-hearted. It is for you, who is struggling to recover from the pain of abuse, you who feel lost in life and deserve some clarity, you who wants to be nurtured to take back control of your life and happiness, and you who want to live a thriving life.

This book is also written with all women, men, and children who are victims of abuse of any kind in mind. It is also for all organisations who are working tirelessly to stop violence in our homes, schools, workplaces, churches, communities and the world. But these organisations can't win this fight if victims/survivors continue to stay with the same mindset. To have a positive result, we need to act differently, and that begins when we choose to turn our pain into gain.

Ten Things This Book Will Help You Accomplish

- **Leave you with greater self-awareness.**
- **Enhance your emotional wellness.**
- **Boost your self-confidence and motivation to bounce back.**
- **Help you unlock your passion and purpose in life.**
- **Support you in setting achievable goals.**

- Help you find clarity and a vision in life.
- Enhance the quality of your personal and work life.
- Get you on your career path.
- Boost the relationship with yourself and loved ones.
- Turn your Pain into Gain.

Five Suggestions on How to Get The Best Out of This Book

1. Everyone is born to live a THRIVING life, and we all have good intentions to be happy. Although we go through emotional and physical pains, they all have a hidden treasure. Thus, the essential approach to reading and understanding this book is by proclaiming with conviction that, "I CAN TURN MY PAIN INTO GAIN". And while YOU read, seek to discover and use the lessons learned from your pain. Let your STRENGTHS become your ANCHOR to a sustainable recovery.

2. The reader would notice that I have consistently used phrases like *"Pain Candidates"* and *"Pain Pals"*. "Pain Candidates" refers to anyone who has experienced or is experiencing emotional or physical pain. "Pain Pals" refers to my acquaintances who have experienced emotional or physical abuse/pain. So, be ready to be part of the conversation.

3. Because this book is thought-provoking, I highly recommend creating a quiet moment where you can absorb the message or statements and reflect on how you can apply them to your life.

4. I would also encourage you to have a pen and a highlighter to highlight statements that are significant to you, and to complete the reflective activities that come with the workbook (Purchased separately).

5. As we all know, repetition makes the information stick. So, endeavour to read the book more than once. And more importantly, apply the principles at every opportunity daily. www.iamthrivingnow.com

Acknowledgement and Appreciations

Throughout my life's journey, there have been some amazing people who have blessed my life, to whom I am so thankful for your love, support, and inspiration. The list is endless and I will name a few.

I wish to say a big THANK YOU

- To God for his Grace and love.
- To my Late Granny (Ma Susan Changsen) for her unfailing love for me.
- To my Mum and family for their prayers, love, and support.
- To my kids for their inspiration and support.
- To Prisca Bamuh for her relentless support.
- To my coach - Christine Gilbert @PLUM HAPPY LIMITED for always believing in me.
- To my Parish Priest – Father Stand for his prayers and support
- To Mr D.Kamara @Dau Services for his enormous contribution
- To Joanne and Laura @ Glow Domestic abuse services for empowering me.
- To all the WOJA sisters @ Women of Justice Arise for standing with me.

- Faith Gakanje @ African Women Empowerment Forum for inspiring me.
- To Sarah Colclough @ Staffordshire Chamber of Commerce for giving me the opportunity to uncover my talent.
- To Mr Tambe Godfrey Egbengip @ One African Foundation for always being there.
- To the Content Editor - Dr Che Bineh for his constant support and guidance.
- To my Public Speaking Coach - Lorna D Sheldon @ LDS(International)limited for helping me to speak with gravitas.
- To Lisa Nichols, Oprah Winfrey and many others, for your inspiration.

Foreword 1

One of the most difficult things to do in life is to be vulnerable and present yourself with such a level of transparency that every scar you once tried to hide is visible for the world to see. That is what you will experience as you read the emotionally written story of *I AM THIRIVING NOW- From a life of Emotional Pain to a Beautiful Life of Freedom.* Peggy Bareh's ability to allow you a glimpse into her emotional past, causes you to reflect on those hidden areas in your life that may have once caused you pain, or they may still be tender spots or even gaping wounds that you try to mend with superficial antidotes. As you follow Peggy, she allows you to step behind the curtain of her heart and see the pain and suffering, yet you find yourself somehow celebrating this heroine of survival. With each step that she takes out of the abyss of brokenness, you can actually feel her heart pounding with new-found confidence and assurance. This read makes you applaud and cheer as you realize that she has transformed from victim into victor.

I must confess that I suffered domestic abuse in my marriage. I did not succumb to the blows of the hand, but to the devasting blows of words that cut and wounded me so badly that I lost my identity. I hid the shame, guilt and tears behind a wide public smile. I did everything that I could to hide my secret from my family and the world. This facade resulted in me becoming a prisoner of my own mind to the point that when I looked in the mirror, I did not recognize the woman staring back at me with lifeless eyes. This beautiful book, I AM THRIVING NOW, would have been a Godsend for me those many years ago. I thank God that my faith, grit, determination, and family support helped me. However, I am so elated that for those who may not have the support networks or know where to turn there is this amazing resource of truth, life, hope and love that is waiting to guide you out of your state of darkness and transform you into the liberated and celebrated being you were meant to be.

Peggy Bareh dared to rise and challenge her thinking. There are those moments that are pivotal and transforming in our lives, and that moment came for Peggy when she read the book *The Power of Your Subconscious Mind* by Joseph Murphy. With a sweeping revelation, she was suddenly propelled into a world of possibilities. Peggy not only realized but accepted and elected to take accountability and responsibility for her own happiness by first doing the work to shift her mindset. Just as Peggy began to think and believe differently and create a new world for herself, you can too.

This book, is truly one of self-discovery with 14 proven steps to help you rediscover your truth, celebrate your authentic self, love yourself and rise like a phoenix with resilient determination to not only survive, but thrive.

I wish you much success, joy, and peace in your life. May you always thrive!

LaWanna Bradford

Chief Operating Officer, The Bradford Group, LLC

Visionary & Founder of Celebrate You Women

Embracing Wellness

Foreword 2

Have you ever found yourself in a place where you feel burdened by the pressure life imposes on you? It could be because of the sadness of loss, the debilitating impact of ill-health, the bewilderment and helplessness of bullying and abuse, or a myriad other reason. You may feel that you're stuck in a situation where there appears to be no way out. You may even have found yourself asking the question, "Why me?" It's understandable that someone in a dire situation may feel that they have become the victim of unbearable circumstances. They feel the weight of anxiety, the emptiness of a lack of energy and the draining impact of helplessness. They may feel that choice has been taken from them. So what can you do about that? The key element here is in recognising that we always have choice. Our uniqueness as living beings on this planet is in our freedom to choose. Let me explain. The power of choice lies in the mindset you adopt as you face that difficult circumstance in your life. There is the mindset of the Victim who says, "This has happened to me and there's nothing I can do about it." Adopting this mindset means that you become stuck in inactivity. However, it is important to recognise that even this represents a choice. Such a person has made the choice to be the victim of their circumstances. Then there is the proactive mindset. Here you accept responsibility for what has happened. Please note, this is not about saying you are to blame for what has happened to you. Blame has no place here. Taking responsibility means actively taking charge of how you respond to your circumstances. This puts you in the place of power over what happens next. And when you are facing terrible circumstances, it means looking at what you can do to make the best of this. What choices can you make? This is the power of the book that Peggy Bareh has created for us. It answers the question of, not just 'How do I survive?', but, most importantly, 'How do I thrive?' When you read more of Peggy's own journey, you realise that here is a woman who thoroughly understands what it means to live with the burden of pressure, right from the earliest days of her life. Her story is as gripping as it is inspirational. As she wisely states, you can't change what has happened to you. The choice lies in what you do next. Peggy demonstrates through her own incredible story, exactly what you can do to bounce back from adversity. She has created a system that guides you through each step of the process. It is like a torch highlighting the route for those who are lost inside the darkness of tragedy and oppression. Page 1 of 2 We can probably be certain that at some point in our life, we will have to face up to adversity. A life without difficulties is an implausible concept. So, when adversity occurs, how do you dig deep into the depths of yourself and find the strength and resilience that will help you to bounce back. Peggy shows us how we can overcome whatever adversity has been placed in our path and learn how to thrive. In this book Peggy holds out her hand to you to support you through your journey. She is the clear embodiment that, with the right mindset, your resilience is a power pack that will lead you back to yourself. Peggy's extraordinary courage and openness in telling her story makes it OK for others to open up about what they are going through. You know that you are not alone. This, in itself, is a great gift that her book offers. So take the hand that Peggy offers and learn how you can gracefully and proactively overcome the adversity and the tragedy you may be facing and, like Peggy, show the world that You Are Thriving Now!

Ruth Driscoll
Toxic Relationship Expert and Creator of
The Life Liberator

Reviews

"This book, is truly one of self-discovery with 14 proven steps to help you rediscover your truth, celebrate your authentic self, love yourself and rise like a phoenix with resilient determination to not only survive, but thrive."

LaWanna Bradford
Chief Operating Officer,
The Bradford Group, LLC
Visionary & Founder of Celebrate You
Women Embracing Wellness

"Peggy's extraordinary courage and openness in telling her story makes it OK for others to open up about what they are going through. You know that you are not alone. This, in itself, is a great gift that her book offers. So take the hand that Peggy offers and learn how you can gracefully and proactively overcome the adversity and the tragedy you may be facing and, like Peggy, show the world that You Are Thriving Now!"

Ruth Driscoll - Driscoll Toxic Relationship
Expert and Creator of The Life Liberator

My Turning Point

....

> "There comes a point where you no longer care
> if there's a light at the end of the tunnel or not.
> You're just sick of the tunnel."
> — Ranata Suzuki

Immediately, on coming out of the school gate, I dashed into my car, feeling the frustration building as I clenched my jaws and felt sick in my stomach. I thought I would explode. With my hands shaking, I gripped the steering wheel and took a deep breath, hoping to drive home safely. As I started driving down my street, I felt choked up and couldn't resist the tears. Storming into the house, I hurried to my bedroom, dropped by my bedside, and with my nails clasped in my hair, I screamed - **"I am fed up! I'm tired! It's not fair! It-is-not-fair!!!"**

Sadly enough, this seemed to have been my usual tormenting feeling and routine after my relationship breakup. It left me disappointed, devastated, angry, and feeling rejected. As I sought refuge in an unfamiliar town, the thought of starting life from scratch was frightening. I wrestled at nights, trying to find comfort from any glimmer of hope, but most times, I lost the fight as my painful memories descended on me like a wolf on its prey. This torturing process went on for over three months, and the physical and psychological impact was written all over me. I didn't dare to look in the mirror for fear of seeing an image of a cranky person with droopy eyelids and pale skin looking back at me. I unconsciously and unhealthily lost approximately one stone. This was due to sleeplessness and loss of appetite. If I had any way to stay locked in my room, that would have been the best option, but my kids needed me.

On this fateful Thursday, I decided to visit my local library to obtain library cards for the kids. While in the queue, the lady in front of me handed in a book she had borrowed. What caught my attention was the bright-yellowish cover. I peered forward to read the title, which read, *"The Power of Your Subconscious Mind"* by Joseph Murphy; out of curiosity, I picked up the book and asked the librarian if I could borrow it. Before she could say, "Sure!", the feeling of emptiness and hopelessness crept in, with a loud voice saying, **"Don't waste your time! That's not going to help you!"** Immediately, I walked off, heading straight to the exit door. But as I pushed opened the second set of doors to come out of the library, another thought popped into my head - "For the very first time in years, you can finally have the time to read again; go get that book." Straight away, I made a U-turn, speeding towards the trolley where I believed the book was. I heaved a sigh of relief when I picked it up, scanned and bagged it. When I got home, instead of lamenting, I started reading. It seemed to me like the content was describing me, outlining all the monster thoughts that were crippling me. From one chapter, I sped through the next, the next and the next, and in three days, I had read the book from cover to cover. One key message I grasped was that "**I own the key to unlocking my happiness, and I just needed to recondition my mind to unlock it.**"

Although it sounded easy, the whole idea seemed impossible. This is because I couldn't figure out how on earth, I could suddenly unlock my happiness just by mental reconditioning. I thought to myself, "If only you knew what I have been through, you would understand that I need more than just reprogramming my mind." Unlocking my happiness was like a jigsaw puzzle for me to assemble, and piecing it together needed me to identify the underlying element that was hindering my happiness. That element was PAIN, and it wasn't as if the pain had just started. Like a ravenous lion hunting for its meal, pain has been chasing me from my childhood. However, at that point, I felt I needed a breakthrough; but how could I do it?

The next morning, after my school drop routine, I came home feeling a bit hopeful but extremely confused – how was I going to rescue myself? The more I thought about it, the more the lousy feeling started swelling up and up until I burst into tears. With a trembling chin and hands, leaking nose and salty drops - all mixed and dripping on the floor, I yelled, "WHY AM I HERE? GOD, WHY WAS I BORN? WHY DIDN'T I DIE THROUGH ALL THOSE PAINS?" And I heard a resounding voice that said, "**Well, those pains happened for a purpose; you needed to grow. You needed to develop the skills and abilities that you'll need to unlock your happiness. And if you could turn that Pain into Gain, you will become the most fulfilled woman on earth.**" And so, beyond my imagination, I successfully turned my Pain into Gain. The journey, however, took some inevitable twists and turns to unlock that door to happiness - a secret I am delighted to share with you.

> *"Life is a combination of lock; your job is to find the right numbers, in the right order, so you can have anything you want"*
> **– Brain Tracy**

"Pain Candidate"

Before we begin to uncover that secret, I would like to ask you some questions. What is it that causes you pain?

Is it the pain of COVID-19, an abusive relationship, a divorce, addictions, rape, societal stigma, discrimination, parenting difficulties, and challenging kids? Or, is it family pressure, business failure, a demanding boss, stressful job, personal failures, obnoxious practices, bereavement, natural disasters or any other? The list can be endless, and my wish for you, the reader, is to update it following your unique painful situation.

I am so glad you're still alive!

What lesson(s) have you learnt from the painful experience(s)?

Is that pain suffocating your growth in any area of your life?

Do you feel that there is more to life than what you currently have?

And finally, do you still want to achieve your dreams in life and be genuinely happy again?

If you have identified your pain(s) and answered yes to any of the questions above, then I welcome you into this Pain *auditorium*; a place where we can, gradually and carefully, unravel the mystery of our pain. I see myself as a *Pain Candidate*[1] and a graduate from *the Pain Institute,* and I am honoured to have you as a partner. I wish to invite you to join me in treading the rocky road of pain, which I am confident will lead to the realisation of our full potential – GAIN.

Pain, I must say, is an essential element of life. It is like the yeast that makes the dough rise, without which the baker won't have the soft, crusty and delicious bread desired.

By the way, what is Pain?

"Pain is an unpleasant sensory and emotional experience associated with actual or potential tissue damage or described in terms of such damage." *(International Association for the Study of Pain - IASP).* Emotional pain could be inflicted by feelings of sadness, stress, anxiety, depression, guilt or shame, fear, low self-esteem, or confidence, etc. Physical pain could be excruciating or burning sensations caused by damage to body tissues, broken bones, injured nerves, and others. From the sources of pain in the opening paragraph, can you identify whether your pain is physical or emotional? Pain, I believe, is innately attached to our lives, like DNA in every human cell, and it's there for a valid reason.

No Pain, No Life

Life has always been painful from birth till this moment. Think about it - for anyone who has endured 'no-epidural'

---

[1] Pain Candidate refers to any victim or survivor of Pain

childbirth. Intense and agonising labour contractions brought us into the world. So, the labour pain is a component of the birth process. As babies, when we came out of the womb or any foetus growth environment, we possibly cried within seconds, minutes, or before our first feed. Luis Villazon mentions that babies may cry "because they are bruised and sore from the trauma of birth..." (BBC Science Focus Magazine)[2] I would also argue that babies feel discomfort because their natural environment (temperature of the womb) has been altered, and they respond by crying.

It is incredible to know that crying, being the first means of expressing human emotion, has become affiliated with pain or discomfort. Even when people shed 'joyful tears,' the thoughts and feelings behind those tears represent relief from a painful position. From our very first cry after birth, we continue crying along our growth journey. When we were hungry, uncomfortable, or wanted attention, we cried! As we crawled, stood, and took our first baby steps, we sustained nasty injuries that caused us to cry! These injuries and discomfort were building blocks for developing the courage to run!

When we started pre-school and primary school, we fell off the scooter, bike, and swings. We had accidents in the playground, sustained burns, food poisoning, and gobbled down nasty stuff. Also, we got bullied and rejected by teachers, friends and families. All these involved pains! As kids, none of these discomforts deterred us except the restriction from our parents or carers. I am sure you were familiar with, "Don't eat that. Don't touch that. Don't do that.

---

[2] https://www.sciencefocus.com/the-human-body/why-do-newborn-babies-cry/

Don't drink that. Don't climb on that! Don't speak to that…"
Also, we can't leave out associated physical and emotional
abuse at the hands of those whom we trusted. Like a dashed
precious artefact, our trust was ruined by those who had no
value in us.

As we continued the pain journey, we then moved on to
teenage and adulthood trauma which, unfortunately, kept
and is still keeping many people hostage, myself included.
As an adult, I have gone through all categories of pain - child
abuse, teenage birth, health issues, obnoxious practices,
societal stigma, rejection, abusive relationships, personal
failures, and grief. My scars are a reminder of those horrifying
moments, which were entirely engulfed by the darkness of
pain. Within that moment of darkness, I found a glimpse of
light, which became a springboard to the journey that turned
my Pain into Gain.

As you will read in Chapter One, I was deemed by many
to have died and come back to life; I indeed did resurrect
from my tomb of pain. If you are one of those who have given
up in life or seemed stuck because you're overwhelmed by a
barrage of painful experiences, then keep reading. I broke out
of that dungeon of the cycle of emotional and physical pain
that incarcerated my life for years. As a *Pain Candidate*, you
will agree with me that it is not a place to be and so you've got
to break out too. An emotional prison cell that seemed like
a thousand metres high, with concrete walls and stainless
steel, guarded 24/7 by armed officers became vincible. In
this book, I will share with you my pain stories. I will also
highlight the reason why I wrote this book and the criteria
you already have to bounce back in life. Lastly, I will share

with you the proven step-by-step approach to turning your Pain into Gain. These are workable principles that helped me and many others to turn our lives around. It will empower you to utilise pain to your advantage. If you're inclined, you will transform that Pain into Gain. You'll bounce back and live the life you have always dreamt of. Let my story be a motivational force to pull you out of your Pain. Let it be a starting point for you to say, "Finally, **I am thriving now.**"

Who would have thought that reading a self-help book like this one would be a turning point in my life?

Chapter 1

The Glimpse of My Pain

*"You care so much you feel as though you will
bleed to death with the pain of it"*
– J.K Rowling.

That faithful sunny afternoon, standing by the lake clasping
my shabby bluish dress in my hands, I shouted, *"**Clodette
Clodette...!**"* but my frantic voice couldn't seem to reach her.
I could see her afloat on the water, a familiar scene reminiscent
of us watching the adults swim side by side with the ducks. It
did not resonate with me that Clodette and I had never gone
into the lake due to prohibition from our parents. I had no
idea why she wasn't responding. Again, the village lake which
was usually busy was deserted on this day, probably because
it was the peak of the farming season and a school day. The
only reason Clodette and I were at the lake instead of being in
the classroom was because we were both labelled 'Obanjeh',
a local term for kids with frequent illness. Skipping school
was normal for us due to recurrent sickness and because

other kids rejected us both at home and in school. Clodette and I bonded and became bosom friends.

As I screamed at the top of my voice, the only answer I got was from a dog, known locally as 'Python'. He came barking fiercely and running around the lake as if he was about to dive in. "What is wrong?" I couldn't stop asking as I wept and called my friend simultaneously. Before I knew it, Python had gripped Clodette by her drenched dress and was swimming across to the lake bank. At last! I could hear human voices and Clodette was out. At age eight, I had no clue what it meant for Python. I didn't know he could swim, let alone save a life. With my bare feet and body, I rushed toward them, hoping to laugh with my only best friend about what I thought was 'an adventure.' But she couldn't respond to me. I dropped on my knees and lifted her right hand, but it flopped on the ground. Then, this man's voice behind me said, "She don die" in the local language, meaning she is dead. What did I even know about death?

The next day, I was admitted to hospital. Was it because of the shock and grief from losing my only friend? I wished I'd had the opportunity to pay her my last respects; if nothing else, I understood the significance. But no, I couldn't. Being in the hospital was my routine from continuous sickness, which led to occasional blackouts. My blackout episodes were sporadic, and no one could tell when this could happen. Nevertheless, the emergency procedure was to use any means available to rush me to the local medical centre, to be strapped in bed with drips injected directly into my veins to revive me. I was lucky to share a single white and rusty hospital bed, with an old plastic spring mattress, which creaked at the slightest movement. Inhaling the foul smell of urine, faeces and medications that saturated the air became familiar. The general statement from the doctors was, "We'll just treat malaria and typhoid." But the cause of the blackouts? - no idea.

Living in a remote village off the northwest of Cameroon, I presume my life was condemned to pain even before I was born. The reason was that, as a toddler, I was left in the care of my maternal granny and life was painful; not because she didn't love me, but because she sacrificed everything to keep me alive. Although my existence became part of her pain, she was delighted to use the pain to bring out the best in me. Part of this was her daily, military-styled calls, commands and training, like, "Come here! Go fetch water! Go harvest vegetables! Go and cook! Go have a watch! Wash the dishes! Go to church! Go to school! Go do this…Go do that!" If I dared to decline any of these instructions, I got punished for it. But the good news about my punishment was that she never laid hands on me because the medical doctors said so. I was too fragile to be beaten. So, I was reprimanded by verbal insults – the kind of disparagement that would leave me weeping for hours until she came and comforted me.

At the age of six, I had learnt to clean, cook and look after myself. During Harmattan, I would trek for miles, braving the dry and dusty wind, to fetch water before I could bathe, cook or drink. I was also obligated to accompany my granny to the farm to be taught the necessary farming skills. At age 7-10, with my usual mysterious episodes in and out of hospital, I was growing and selling vegetables to afford essential items like books, pencils, clothes, flip-flops, and even school fees. Farming, which was often done under heavy rain or scorching sun, was the only mode for survival.

If I had only had to deal with the pain of poverty, insults, and rejection, I would have been a satisfied child. Besides these, I was born with a 'mysterious disease' which even the medical team at my local hospital had no clue about. My medical condition became dreadful and unexplainable to people. I was regarded as a 'mysterious being' because one minute I was perfectly fine and the next minute, the whole community would be screaming... "She don die!" After this, I was in hospital, and then I was back home! People even nicknamed me 'half die' meaning, 'half-dead or walking dead.' My fragility could be easily spotted from my petite, pale, and tired appearance. As a result, most parents vehemently warned their kids not to come near me because I could drop dead at any time, and nobody wanted to take the blame. The only friend I had – Clodette, who herself had health issues - unfortunately, drowned before my own eyes. The rejection from the kids in the community was painful, and that compelled me to be attached to my granny, my garden, my pencil, and some scrapped papers for writing anything I could think of.

I dreaded going to school because anyone could kick, punch, boss me around and even seize my homemade packed lunch. Nevertheless, the bullying and stigma didn't deter me because that's the only place I could learn to read and write. One thing I wished was for me to be a "normal" child, but could that be possible?

The Obnoxious Alternative

With modern medical diagnosis giving no hope, my granny resorted to traditional treatment which was another painful experience. According to the verdict of the traditional doctors, my heart had been eaten or stolen by witches and wizards. Even though my granny never believed in superstitions, she was at the crossroads because, at that moment, she just wanted to save my life.

Packing a few clothes and food items, not enough to last me for six months, granny held my hands, and we set off on our 12-mile journey on foot to a treatment centre. Under the blazing sun, using a tiny footpath, we journeyed through tall bushes and forest. I couldn't ignore the creaking of trees, whistling wind, rustling leaves and chirping birds. Halting twice to eat, rehydrate and rest my feeble 10-year-old legs, we finally arrived. At once, I spotted a scruffy and muscular middle-aged man of about 5ft 8inches. With cheerfulness and optimism, my granny greeted the traditional doctor, "I Salute Baba!", and we were ushered into the treatment room.

The room was approximately two times the size of an average living room, with walls constructed from bamboo, a thatched roof, a bamboo door and two windows. Within it were about ten single bamboo beds with grass mattresses, and no bedding, each allocated to a patient. All the ten bed spaces were full, which meant that Granny and I needed to sleep on the dusty floor until an extra bed was provided. In the back garden was a range of farm animals generating unattended waste which made the place stunk. With no toilets and bathrooms, the patients used nearby bushes as lavatories and washed in the open air.

The traditional treatment of my heart malfunction was to begin the next day for about six months, and it involved a combination of approaches. The first approach required me to eat animal hearts. At midday, a goat was slaughtered in front of me. With blood gushing and sprinkling on my clothes as the defenceless animal fought and jerked, the chest was instantly ripped, and the beating heart removed and diced for me to swallow with fermented palm juice. With a disgusted and scrunched up face, I burst into tears. Simultaneously, the doctor and my granny yelled at me to **"take and drink!"** Reluctantly stretching my shaking hands, I grabbed the drink and slowly opened my mouth for the raw blood-dripping heart to be shoved in. With dirty and bloodied hands, the doctor forced a piece in my mouth, took the drink from my hand and poured it in. I did my best to swallow, but immediately threw up, emptying my stomach. Out of the half-digested food, mixed with stomach fluids, he picked up the rejected piece of heart and forced me to swallow again! This taunting procedure repeated each morning, gulping the remaining heart until there was a need to kill another animal. According to the traditional practitioners, it would replace my stolen heart.

The second method of treatment involved standing stripped for incisions to be done on my chest by use of a razor blade. I became familiar with the hostile instructions from the traditional Doctor like, "Come here! Take your clothes off and hold these two spears." As I gripped onto both spears, one on each hand, I could feel the blade slicing into my ill-stricken and bony chest. *"Ouchhh!!... Ouchhh!!... Ma, Help Me!!... Help Me!!"* I cried calling my granny, who also sat with tears in her eyes, helplessly peering at me. I could feel the blood dripping from my chest to my feet. After the incision, the fresh wound was brushed with some green concoction, which itself was burning like very hot chilli. All this while, I was still holding onto the spears with my arms stretched out and shaking. This obnoxious alternative and painful routine was carried out twice a week for nearly a year, as six months wasn't enough. During those moments, I begged for death, but death didn't come. I couldn't bear the pain anymore.

As nothing seemed to work, my grandma eventually got fed up and took me back home. It was great to be home, although a lot of cleaning was required to make the house, abandoned for 8 months, habitable. Nothing had changed about my health; it was deteriorating. Had Granny given up? Absolutely not. This time, she sold all her valuables, borrowed money from the church, and took me to a bigger hospital in another city. Living in the city with no means of income to meet the endless hospital bills required us to stay with some relatives, and for granny to do odd jobs to raise money. After ten months of constant hospital referrals and granny's inability to foot the bills, I was finally medically diagnosed with aortic valve regurgitation or leaking valve. Supposedly, that explained the cause of my blackouts and frequent hospital admissions. My granny received the news with such glee as if she had just won the jackpot. I was prescribed an extencilline injection to be administered each month until I was 26 years old. Granny and I did our best to follow the prescription regimentally for nearly three years. However, when the cost of the medication increased from about £2 – £4 at the time, we couldn't afford it and so I stopped. But luckily, I was feeling much healthier; no more passing out, although I frequently still had swollen feet, heart palpitations, and chest pain. Through all of these, I did all I could to be educated, apart from missing a whole academic year from transiting from the obnoxious treatment to my saving grace treatment.

While Granny and I were away for nearly a year, news reached her relatives that I was dead and buried. There was no phone or social media for accessible communication as we have today. And so, my granny's relatives performed a traditional funeral for me. To my granny and everyone in my community, returning home healthier felt like I had indeed risen from the dead. All I needed was to reward her someday for all the sacrifices, but was that going to happen?

I Lost My Heroine

I admired my granny for her bravery, tenacity, and outstanding achievements in every sphere of her life. To me, she was my hero. She was a woman of justice and did everything in her capacity to save not just my life, but those of others – even strangers. She was highly revered within the community for her noble qualities. I always ran to her for physical and emotional comfort, and she never once let me down. Her dream was to find me a place of safety, free from emotional and physical pain – a place of inner serenity.

As a way of safeguarding me when I was 15, my granny wanted me to join the convent as a nun. She didn't want any man to hurt me after all I had endured. Secondly, many people believed that I wasn't ever going to have a child due to my health condition. But I refused because I had always dreamt of falling in love, being a wife, and having kids. I was feeling very well in myself and lived like any other teenager. I also wanted a relationship – someone who would love me, irrespective of my pains in life. Besides, I wanted to play with my kids, talk with them, walk them to school, take them shopping and spend quality time together. These are the experiences that I missed growing up. After convincing my granny, her only wish was to embrace my child someday as proof of her relentless sacrifice to give me my dream. On my part, I promised to repay her sacrifices once I graduate from college and hopefully got a job. Sadly, she died too soon, dashing all my hopes of putting a smile on her face.

After a couple of years, I finally got married and was happy because I knew I had found someone to spend the rest of my life with. The thought of my painful experiences aroused trauma that could affect my future. As a solution, I fought hard to shut the door of my painful past and open a new chapter in life - to love and be loved. Did I get it?

When Love Turns Into Hatred

The moment we spoke on the phone, the evidence was clear – there was an unexplainable connection – I felt the warmth. He was soft-spoken, level-headed, spiritual, romantic, intelligent and sincere. As I ended the call, I felt the surge of mixed feelings; the sense of euphoria, excitement and scepticism engulfed me. "He's loving! Is he different? Will I be hurt?" were some of my endless questions. The more we spoke, the more doubt vanished and the feeling of "I finally found my companion" grew even stronger. We couldn't wait to meet physically, and I told myself that "my love for him will be beyond looks, charm and accomplishments". I was ready to bear it all for the sake of love. When we finally met, it felt like we had known each other for years and with no hindering thoughts, we needed to get the ball rolling. He proposed, and I said yes! Within no time, we met both families and friends, each throwing in their support, except for a disgruntled few. But who really cared? Love was the watchword, and nothing could beat it. What was the meaning of emotional or healthy boundaries? I had no clue and didn't even think I needed one because love transcended everything.

I enjoyed my married life. I loved and felt loved. Everything was smooth from the beginning, as my spouse supported me, educated me, and I looked up to him as my mentor and put him on a pedestal. Just at a time when I thought I had achieved my dream of a loving home, pain struck again. Communication, intimacy, attention, warmth, appreciation, empathy, reassurance, honesty, openness, common sense, respect and care seemed to have been flung through the window. The layers of emotional protection were being chipped away, and I watched, with anguish, my loving home gradually turning into an unhappy home. The love we once shared turned into hatred. Once more, the painful feeling of rejection, loneliness, grief, depression and failure gripped and immobilised me. All attempts to resolve our marital challenges failed. "Was there anything I wasn't doing right?" was one of the hundred questions

I asked myself. I resorted to using all mechanisms – sensible and foolish ones - to communicate my fragility, to relieve the situation and to prove my loyalty and love for my spouse. But the more I tried, the more I felt rejected, and the atmosphere was physically and emotionally draining for everyone. Watching the glaring message of dissatisfaction on the face of my partner was heart-breaking, and it left me in confusion and constant worry. If there was any magic button to reset the relationship, that would have been the best thing ever! But no, there wasn't. I suddenly realized that I had invested my time and energy in meeting unending goal posts and mitigating an emotional cold war that was also impacting the kids. The whole situation was a mess, and I must admit it was more painful than watching my best friend drown. It was more painful than swallowing animal hearts and getting my chest chopped, and even more painful than losing my granny.

I couldn't cope with the exhaustion and the strain it was putting on my health. Luckily, this time I had the right medical team and I had to undergo open-heart surgery to replace my aortic valve with a mechanical valve. Laying on the surgical bed and speaking with the hospital porter and my partner, as I was wheeled into the operating theatre, I couldn't help reflecting on what had preoccupied my mind for weeks. As if I were saying my last prayer, I told myself that, "I love my kids, I love my partner, I love my family, but maybe granny loves me more and would want me to join her…" After about seven intensive hours of the surgery, I made it through, and I am stronger than ever before.

Love Will Cause You to Let Go

After resisting demands to leave for so long, I finally left my relationship with our three kids because we all needed some emotional stability. We hear statements like, "If you truly love him/her, you'll endure any pain till death do you part." But I dare to differ because I wouldn't want anyone dead. Instead, true love will let you leave or lose the other half of you if doing so would make the other happy. That was a courageous decision and a significant turning point in my life. And when I left, I knew that was the end of my life because I was made to believe that I was a failure. I began as a good wife and a good mother, but constant happenings within the relationship made me believe that I was a bad wife and mom. This led to my belief that I was a failure because it was echoed to me daily. This also affected my thoughts, and I lost my confidence as a good mother and a good wife, and my aspiration to be an entrepreneur seemed impossible because of my self-imposed limitations. I felt useless, and my self-confidence was at zero. I am very sure you too may have been in a similar situation.

However, after reflecting on my life and who I am, I realized that the only way I could change my life was to do one thing. For me, that one thing was to SEE MY PAIN AS A FOUNDATION TO GROWTH. Thus, my pain had a hidden treasure. Like I mentioned at the beginning, I was instigated by an inner voice to understand that I had gone through enough pain, and if I could turn that PAIN into GAIN, I would become the most fulfilled woman on earth. This one thought changed my whole life, and this now leads me to share with you how this book came about.

CHAPTER 2

Where It All Started

....

*"No one is useless in this world who lightens the
burdens of another"*
— Charles Dickens

Here I was, sitting in a workshop full of pain; everyone around me was feeling the burden of some form of torture. Alas, I found other *Pain Candidates*, each one narrating their painful experiences, cross-talking and trying to release years of bottled-up agonies. To most of the *Pain Candidates*, we were very skilful in recounting our pains because it was second nature. With years of experience, we couldn't go wrong about it.

My quest for changing my life motivated me to search for recovery and empowerment programs within my community. Although I had started reading self-help books, attending workshops like this was pivotal for my personal growth. Nothing could be more relieving than sitting in a room with like-minded candidates. As the back-and-forth chattering was getting more intense, I decided to stay silent as Meg, one participant, tearfully seized the scene with her dreadful experience. *"I trusted him!"* she yelled and then continued. "He was my best friend. I went to him for everything - advice, a walk in the park and playtime. He promised to protect me and never to hurt me. They called me, 'his baby girl' because of our closeness. I admired him, and I was also excited to get a nice man like him when I *grew up. But these all changed the morning I found myself bleeding profusely from my intimate part, not knowing what had happened. The burning sensation, abdominal cramp, and the rest were gruesome! I couldn't stop asking what happened, when, and how? The last thing I remembered from the night before was that my dad put me to sleep after reading my favourite story. At that moment, I missed my mum! I had always asked my dad why my mum wasn't living with us, and he always said I wouldn't understand. But I didn't feel much of her absence because my dad gave me everything I needed, and I trusted him. The pain couldn't stop me from thinking. I remembered what my teacher had taught me during our sex education lessons. Did someone pull my pants? I pondered, feeling confused because my dad said I could be menstruating. He declined my request to see the GP and made me believe that I was having 'girly issues'. He cuddled me up and gave me a warm water bottle to soothe the cramp. After three days, the pain was relieved, and I was back in school. This incident occurred every three weeks for nearly a year, and I had no idea that I was being raped by my dad, whom I loved and trusted. I was sedated with my favourite drink every Friday during our popcorn movie night. With that emotional scar, my life has never been the same because of that monster..."*

The whole group cried as she painfully narrated her ordeal. We all had a 10-minute break for a brew, fresh air, and some nicotine for those who needed it. As for me, I sat glued to my seat, lost in profound thoughts. Have you ever been in a position where, after listening to someone's painful story, you feel like yours is trivial? That's the same way I felt. I listened as others narrated their painful trail; some showed stabbed wounds, scars, dislocated bone, chipped tooth - you name it. The participants then switched to identifying all the impacts of these pains. The similar painful consequences were depression, anxiety, fear, bipolar disorder, addiction, disability, guilt, lack of trust, resentment, loss of freedom, low self-esteem, lack of confidence, traumatized children, lost careers, financial hardship, lost homes and belongings, and the list goes on.

One thing I became aware of during such meetings, which at first wasn't welcomed by my *pain pals*[3], was my optimism – thanks to my faith, reading books and watching videos of motivational speakers. Each time I opened my mouth to contribute, I looked at the positive of my pain even though I was also suffering from fear, financial hardship, passiveness, and low self-esteem. As the negative-impact exercise continued, the trainer finally broke the cycle and asked, "What are some of the good things you have benefited from through these experiences?" And the whole room went silent. "Yes! This is my turn to speak", I muttered to myself as I scribbled in my book. After I had finished, I used my pen to draw a square around it, and I called it my:

Strength Toolbox (STB)

For most participants, it was easier to come up with an endless negative list of their pains than a positive one. "Okay,

---

[3] Pain pals refers to my friends who are victims or survivors of abuse

can I start?" I asked the trainer, and with her approval, I opened my 'STB.' "Thanks to my painful experiences, I have learned to: Be an independent person, a good cook, a good cleaner, sing, love myself, love writing, value life, share, be hardworking, disciplined, resilient, patient, loving, caring, empathetic, ambitious, appreciative, listen, easily forgiving …" The list was endless, and it seemed to have awakened the brain of my *pain pals* as they started nodding their heads in affirmation and scribbling theirs. One said, "Yeah, thinking about it, I didn't realise how much I had learned from my abusive mother…I am courageous, creative, vigilant and, I guess, very organised too…" With my hand raised, I reiterated to the trainer that, "our strengths become our greatest tools to utilize whenever we're faced with challenges and they must NEVER be minimised." As others were listing their strengths, I was physically present, but my mind was concentrating on something else. "What could that be?" you may ask. To me, I was convinced that life would be incomplete without implementing what I was thinking.

Leaving such gatherings made me feel so blessed to have created a positive network with survivors like me. It made me understand that I wasn't alone. The experiences of pain might look and sound different, feel in varying degrees – low, medium, and high, but they're all PAIN! They all hurt physically and psychologically. However, there was something that needed to be done which kept me restless.

"Our strengths become our greatest tools to
utilize whenever we're faced with challenges.
So, they must NEVER be minimised."

The Many Questions

My interaction with my *Pain pals* indicated that we all had the power to bounce back, so why couldn't we? Why had many people in that room felt so demotivated about life? Even those that had moved on; why did they keep relapsing into their pain cycle? Why were many of us not living the life we had always dreamt of? Why were many of us still letting our painful experiences rule our lives? These and many more questions couldn't stop bucking in my mind.

In that training room, I could see and feel the positive energy vibrating from what I would call "Heroes of Pain" – Real Fighters and Survivors. That's right! We fought pain and triumphed, that's why we're still **ALIVE!** I could see future movers and shakers; the best of the best in all fields and expertise: Entrepreneurs, Motivational speakers, Authors, Ministers, Presidents, Bankers, Support workers, Lawyers, Nurses, Engineers, Managers, Doctors, Teachers, Singers, Accountants, Counsellors, just to name a few. I could see the world of pain crushing down because these 'Best Minds' were audaciously embarking on using their *Pain Strengths* to change their lives. Yes! The pain will be crushed because each pain comes with its antidote, which I will talk about later. But what I perceived as the issue was that, *Pain Candidates* often seem to focus and ruminate on the pain, while negating the antidotes. At least, that is one thing I was smart enough to capture, which made me sound more optimistic than others in such gatherings. I had made a promise to myself that whichever recovery training I attended, I would do my utmost to project positivity. In one of those training sessions, it didn't initially

occur to me that the way I viewed and spoke about my pain
was making any difference to my *pain pals*. However, that
perception changed when I received my little 'who I am box.'

Who I am Box

At the end of one such recovery training, all participants were
presented with a little heart-shaped box. Participants were
each given a blank note pad to write what they thought about
each person in the group and put them in the boxes. When
I opened my box - Behold! Here is what I found.

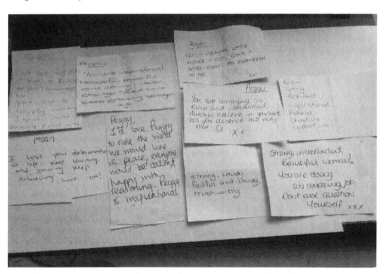

FIG 0.1: My Unrecognized Strengths

When we met at the next training session, I could see and
sense something different in the training room. I could sense
the feeling of relief, confidence, hope, optimism, and only
God knows what others had written about each candidate.
I wrote inspiring and motivating messages to each candidate,

encouraging them to use their hidden strengths to their benefits. As we were relaxing over tea and coffee, Linda, one of the participants, pulled towards me and applauded me for being so serene, wise, and optimistic. She went on and on without giving me the chance to praise her too. She then said,

> "I would like to be mentally resilient like you. I want to bounce back. I don't like this **Shit** life I'm living. **This is not me!!** I just want to leave the pain behind and move forward without limiting myself. But how do I do that? Peggy, how did you do it? I have just one kid and look at me. **I am wrecked!** My son is also wrecked; his confidence is gone. But look at you, *you're a single mum with three 'bloody' kids … Two teenagers for that matter, and each time I see you, you appear as calm, presentable, articulate, optimistic… You look as if you have no issues! Thank goodness for these training sessions, otherwise, my life would have been worse than this. While we talk about how to barely survive with our lives, you talk about your future business and dreams… How do you do it? Please, I want to know…"*

Phew! If I told you that I knew the answer off the top of my head, I would be lying. The intensity of her quest to understand my so-called 'little secret' drove me blank. All I could do is give her a big, tight, and long hug and assured her that I would return with an answer to her question. Honestly, throughout that training session, my whole mind was on Linda's question; **"Peggy, how did you do it?"** I said to myself, "She was absolutely right! How do we bounce back after experiencing painful events in our lives? Yes, we have the knowledge, experiences, and strengths to move on, but **how do we use them?**" I thought to myself, "The **'how'** may be the missing piece of the puzzle in our journey of lasting recovery."

I knew I had done something to bounce back and be focused; I read many books, did my research, attended workshops and seminars, spoke to other survivors and created my own recovery strategy. Yet, I never had the thought and time to capture them to help others. I thought to myself, "Can this be the 'little secret' that could help Linda and others to achieve a lasting recovery?" This led me to a re-reflection on my past experiences; how I felt when I reached my breaking point. That moment when I felt like Linda. Also, that moment when I told myself that I had endured enough pain, and it was time to move on! It led me to reflect on how I felt and what I did to move out of my naiveté. These memories reignited anger, frustration and grief, but I had to endure once more for the sake of Linda. Her words and requests became a foundation and a source of strength for me. From that position, I felt I was resilient and useful enough to others, although I knew I was still struggling to get to full recovery. Tapping into my experiences, knowledge, strengths and all the transformational resources (books and training), I began writing this book to help Linda and you, the reader, to **Turn Your Pain into Gain and live a Thriving Life.** This book is written on the basis that:

> *Most people go through painful experiences in life which also come with lessons that can help in growth and recovery. So, what are the lessons we learn from*

our painful experiences? How do we use the lessons
learnt? What processes or resources are available to
enable us to use our painful experiences as a lesson
for future growth and recovery?

Turning pain into gain means turning your problems
into solutions; turning your pain into passion and helping
someone; turning your weaknesses into strengths and turning
your strengths into an anchor to thrive in life. Turning pain
into gain also means acknowledging that suffering is part of
life and has lessons that can propel us to future growth; that
accepting pain is the first step to learning and developing a
way to overcome it; that it is after we go through suffering
that we can effectively manage our weaknesses as a source of
strength; that acknowledging our contributions in the pain
process is a steppingstone to growth and recovery. Turning
pain into gain involves an honest evaluation of our actions in
life towards our friends, family, partners or co-workers and
the effects on our future. It also involves our willingness to
redefine who we are which then leads to a fruitful future…
sounds so crazy, eh? It will become clearer and transformative
as you read on.

When I said that every pain brings its antidote, it wasn't
an overstatement. For example, if you have always been
passive and letting people take advantage of you, what do
you need to do? You would need to learn to be assertive and
get your needs met. Once that is done, your passiveness has
brought you assertiveness, and you're now happy because
your needs are met! You just turned that pain into gain.
So, every suffering produces its solution if only we choose

to act on it. It is there for our growth and happiness. Now you could be asking yourself, "How is this assault, trauma, abuse, physical and emotional pain meant for my growth and happiness? How is it possible that my agony is meant for my growth?" We'll find out as we read further.

Looking at the above example, it sounds easy, right? But unfortunately, it's not, especially coming from a place of prolonged pain. When your life has been wrecked, your mental health affected, your confidence gone, your self-esteem ripped off, your trust damaged, your physical strength sapped, your motivation deprived, your optimism gone and your emotions detached, letting go can be difficult. Rising and taking new steps is tough and flipping your agony into progress is debilitating. It takes one into a position of darkness and total blackout which, if not properly handled, may lead to more disastrous and devastating situations. I hope that walking through these conversations and participating with honesty will provide a clear path to bringing light into our darkness, **thus, providing us with a platform to begin our healing, recovery, and growth process.** There is no point worrying about how the pain came about; that is history. All that matters now is your happiness and how to get there. You need to focus on regaining that happiness you enjoyed before the unfortunate pain took it away. This is possible if we begin by identifying the positive lessons of our pains and the appropriate means to establish the antidotes. This premise builds on the fact that many get utterly immersed in pain and give up on life or get confused about what the future might hold for them. Identifying the positives or what we could have done better to avoid our pain begins the process of turning the pain into gain.

> **Every suffering produces its solution if only we choose to act on it. It is there for our growth and happiness.**

We too can have 'A CLIMB' to reach our highest potential in life

As you will read in Chapter 16, my vision to transform my pain into gain led me to study the lives of some most successful and fulfilled personalities like Oprah Winfrey, Gordon Ramsay, J.K Rowling, Lisa Nichols, Jack Canfield, Kathryn Joosten, and Tony Robbins, to name a few. My interest was on how they became fulfilled in life and commanded a considerable following. I was interested in the way they leverage their challenges and strengths, and today, are helping others overcome their difficulties. They all went through pain! But they turned their pain into gain, reached their highest potential and are living their dream lives. So, what is stopping us from living our own dream lives? Do we have what it takes to climb to our highest potential?

'A CLIMB' is an acronym which I created as criteria for our recovery road map - **I AM THRIVING NOW.**

'A CLIMB' stands for:

- **A** - Alive
- **C** - Contact with pain
- **L** - Learn from pain

- **I** - Inclination or willingness to change
- **M** - Movement or road map
- **B** - Bounce back

Our journey to turning our pain into gain might sound like a highly skilled job offer. Before an employer offers a job to an employee, the employee must have met specific job criteria. For example, physically present, have skills and experiences needed for the job role, willing to learn and climb their career ladder, and achieve their dream.

We, *Pain Candidates* can also accomplish our dreams because we meet the bounce back criteria, which are the first three elements.

1. **We are still alive!** Or physically present.
2. **We have had contact with or experienced the pain.** Hence, we have the skills.
3. **We have learned from the pain.** Hence, willing to move on.
4. **Are we willing to thrive?** The answer to this will be subjective, and without the inner drive to change your life, you may find it challenging to get to B (bounce back). As *Pain Candidates*, we might prefer our comfort zones and don't want to change. That's why we talk, and complain, and yet do nothing about it. However, once you decide to come out of your comfort zone, you'll be halfway on the journey to bouncing back.
5. **Are we ready to follow a road map to bounce back?** Again, this answer is personal based on your response to question 4. Someone like Linda will be very excited

to follow the road map because it is the answer to her question, "How did you do it?"

6. **Bounce back!** This will be your result if you're willing to change your life and follow the step-by-step recovery approach or road map below.

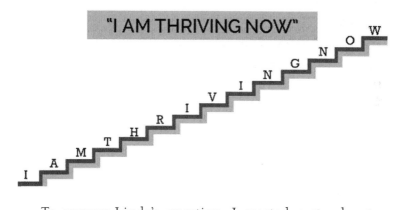

To answer Linda's question, I created a step-by-step recovery and empowering approach to bouncing back to life. This is the same formula I used which helped me to be serene, optimistic, focused, ambitious, objective, assertive, create healthy habits, change my mindset, manage my time, have a meaningful life, and achieve my dreams. It helped me to turn my pain into gain.

Life is at its best when we all aim to THRIVE in whatever area we choose. When we thrive, we become fulfilled. In my view, there is no middle ground. Either we are living a fulfilled life, or we are not. We can't be in between. We live accomplished lives when we achieve our goals in life and the desire to have a thriving life is personal. If we choose to stay in our current position, we can. If we decide to move, we also can! Interestingly, success is non-discriminatory if its principles are applied. So, it doesn't matter who you are and what you've been through; if you believe that you can still be successful, you can! Just like me and many others who did bounce back to life, I hope this recovery road map can also help you to turn your pain into gain and bounce back. But first, you need to ignite your mindfulness to the desire to change – which we'll be sharing in the next chapter. Like a tortoise, I had unconsciously slept long enough in my discomfort, and it was beginning to impinge on every area of my life. Without a shadow of a doubt, it was time for me to wake up!

The desire to have a thriving life is personal.
If we choose to stay in our current position,
we can. If we decide to move, we also can!

CHAPTER 3

Step 1: Ignite Mindfulness

*"I will not let anyone walk through my mind with
their dirty feet."*
– Mahatma Gandhi

Should you continue to sleep through the pain or choose to wake up?

Imagine that the physical assault and emotional manipulation have been occurring over and over; the "I am sorry, it won't happen again" has been repeated countless times; the passiveness and "I forgive you" have become a daily routine, and the "devastated and broken You" seems trapped. What should you do? Continue to sleep or wake up?

As *Pain Candidates*, we're not usually happy with the status quo, yet we remain in denial of the situation or in denial of our strengths to thrive. We refuse to embrace what it takes to make us happy and refuse to believe that we can still bounce back. We also allow people to continue walking through our minds with their dirty feet. Because we "sleep" through the pain, our growth and happiness are deprived. That's why it is vital that we ignite our consciousness – wake up!

For many *Pain Candidates*, the need to change doesn't always come as a priority. Most, at times, underestimate our potential and our wealth of skills, making them more dormant, thus hindering our abilities to grow. Our pain experiences, therefore, act as a hindrance and deter our abilities to thrive. Also, we have become complacent to our pain and have accepted living with it, thus making us dishonest with our predicaments. When people ask, "how are you doing?" Our response is, "I am fine", even when we know we're not. Our complacency breathes some air of 'faux comfort' which assures us of survival in the 'dragon's den,' and disables our move towards restoration or recovery. That's the moment when we tell people, "I don't need your help. I can survive it", although deep down, we know we can't.

Furthermore, we often use contentment as a defence mechanism, making statements like, "I am lucky to have a partner", even when the partner has chosen to become a thorn in the flesh. When we become afraid of losing our self-control and our limiting beliefs, we continue to downplay the existence of the pain. This happens especially in our relationships where we feel like we're in control of the situation. This holds the same for other abusive or painful conditions like illness, addiction, mental health, financial problems, work challenges etc. Whenever we reject the existence of abuse or pain, we are unconsciously rejecting the need to change and move towards recovery. We could end up developing the attitude of shifting blame or having genuine reasons for every action. This may include refusing to accept or even change our negative behaviours because we become blind to our weaknesses. However, the truth remains that, if we want to move from where we are to where we want to be, we must accept the present reality. And the reality is that we must ignite consciousness of our pain and be willing to turn it into gain. Covid-19 has inflicted more pain, and many seem to be giving up hope. It's time to tell yourself that, "This is enough! I have had enough, and it is time to still dream, step forward and live my dreams".

In my experience, I dreamt of becoming an entrepreneur, a life coach, a motivational speaker, a philanthropist, be in a loving and happy relationship, spending some quality time with my kids and others. For Linda, she dreamt of becoming assertive, going back to college, and obtaining her degree as a beautician. What is your dream? Is it to:

- Change that stressful job?
- Make some more money?
- Lose that weight?
- Have a new relationship?
- Stop that addiction?
- Come out of that depressive state?
- Become a parent?
- Travel the world?
- Or what is it?

> Whenever we reject the existence of abuse or
> pain, we are unconsciously rejecting the need
> to change and move towards recovery.

We Always Know What We Want

Have you noticed that whenever you ask a family member, friend, or colleague what they want in life, they would always have an answer? For some, their dream may be as simple as learning to cook a specific meal. For others, it could be learning to drive, or learning to play a piano or sing, ending that abusive relationship, and so on. For others, it might be owning their own home, their own business, having a highly skilled job, travelling the world, becoming a philanthropist, etc. If you ask them the steps taken to achieve that dream, you will also get varied answers. They might say, "I am doing nothing" or "It's not the right time for me". That is when you get all the "if only," "I can't" and "Because" statements like:

- If only I had the money, I would start my driving lessons…
- If only I can come out of this depression, I will socialise…
- If only I had the time, I would take piano lessons…
- If only my kids were grown, I would start college…
- I can't travel because …
- I can't sing because …
- I can't leave because…
- I can't find a job because…
- I can't own my own business because…

I must admit that having been in this state myself, we might sometimes have genuine reasons or barriers why we can't achieve what we want, especially health barriers. Just like we don't know what we don't know, we also can't do what we can't do! Though, sometimes the problem is not because we genuinely can't do it, but rather because we **do not want to leave our comfort zones**. I am sure you would agree that the frightening thought of moving or changing our current environment, status, and state of mind becomes a massive barrier to turning our pain into gain. Your comfort zone may just be aggravating the pain.

The Pain of a Comfort Zone

Show me someone who doesn't have a comfort zone, and I will tell you that they only just stretched their comfort zone.

We all have our environmental and mental comfort zones. These are our boundaries; what we can tolerate and what makes us feel safe or at ease. Athletic champions, celebrities, political figures, professionals and others, are just what they are because they stretch their comfort zones. Just like baby zoo elephants, who, from birth, are usually mentally trained to a specific confine, we too are tamed in the same way. When we were born, we were taught to think, talk, and behave like our trainers (parents or guardians). We followed the rules and regulations, and anything out of the ordinary was considered inappropriate.

I grew up with the mindset of poverty, self-reliance, working hard, and obedience. I thought money and a thriving life was meant only for a specified category of people. From childhood, I repeatedly heard the quote, *"Money is the root of all evils"* and so I didn't want to be evil. That also prevented me from stretching myself to be financially comfortable, which would have enabled me to live a thriving life. I was busy working harder and barely struggling to survive from paycheque to paycheque, rather than investing in myself and working smarter. I thought it was wrong to ask others for help or to say no to people's requests. So, I didn't mind becoming the 'Jack of all trades' just because I was afraid to ask for help. I was comfortable saying yes all the time because I didn't want to upset anyone. And I carried this mindset into my relationship, avoiding any situation that would make me feel uncomfortable.

For us, *Pain Candidates*, our comfort zones are usually 'comfortable' but also painful! I naively thought my passiveness, self-reliance, and obedience would keep me safe and in control of my values and emotions; instead, they left me vulnerable. I couldn't stand up for myself or ask for my needs with confidence. Also, I was constantly taking the blame because that felt safer for me. Being financially stretched and trying to do everything alone was exhausting! But the thought of exiting my mental conditioning, setting boundaries or asking for my needs was painful! The more I stayed in that comfort-pain zone, the more I became tamed; comfortable with my painful experiences and mindset; comfortable to hold the physical and mental spears in each hand and let people slice me as they wanted; comfortable to keep running around like a 'headless chicken', and feeling obligated to satisfy everyone, except myself. Each time we think of doing something different from our usual way of life, we become very uncomfortable.

Everything you are currently experiencing right now in your life is within your comfort zone. Your way of thinking, talking, and behaving; the level of your self-esteem and confidence; your lifestyle (healthy or unhealthy); the jobs and responsibilities you accept; the friends and places you visit; your financial status and spending habits; your health, fitness, and your home; your parenting style and hobbies, and the list goes on. We have been placed in our "TED Talk" Circle of pain for too long and breaking out is paramount.

My "TED Talk" Circle

As I mentioned earlier, everyone has a comfort zone. Some people's comfort zones are narrower than those of others, based on choice. If you've ever watched "TED talk," you would surely have noticed that the speakers normally stand within a circle throughout their speech. But others may consciously or unconsciously step out of the ring. I understand that the rule is for speakers to try and stay within that circle for varied reasons. However, there's usually no distinct reward for staying within the circle, neither is there any penalty for stepping out of it (well, so long as the speaker doesn't wander too far off from lighting). Nevertheless, if a speaker wanders off and delivers a powerful message, would the audience care if he stepped out of the circle?

Our comfort zone is like our own "TED Talk" circle. But thankfully, we are not obliged to stay within the circle. Luckily, we're not tethered like the baby elephant to remain within a defined space – we're free to move away from our circle, as far away as we want. We're also privileged as human beings, to change our neural pathways. It doesn't matter what we picked from our growth environments and the way our brains were programmed. It doesn't matter the painful experiences we went through. It also doesn't matter our present circumstances. What matters is whether we are willing to change our mental programming. You can choose how you want to think, talk, and behave. You're not compelled to follow what others demand of you. As a unique being, you have your ambitions in life and what brings you joy, and so it is your choice to shoot for that dream.

Remember the dream you mentioned at the start of this chapter? That dream is out of your comfort zone and to achieve that dream would require you to stretch your circle. We need to be comfortable to be uncomfortable in our 'comfort-pain zone.' It is fine to step out of the ring if it is inconvenient for us. After all, it's not an offense. The only way I could turn the pain from my comfort zone into gain was to use its antidote. In order to fight passiveness, I needed to be assertive. It was vital to learn that asking was my right, and so it was ok to ask others for help; it was ok to voice my feelings. I had to learn that it's fine to say no to people's requests. I also learned that it was ok to make mistakes and not be crippled by guilt. Moreover, I learned not to accept responsibility for people's abusive behaviour, but rather to take responsibility for my happiness. By doing so, I stretched my comfort zone, which helped me to become the best version of myself. Perhaps you're the type that feels paralysed with anxiety or depressed whenever you think of doing something that will take you out of your comfort zone. The good news is that by stretching yourself just by an inch towards the right direction, you'll be starting your success journey. You don't need a massive jump; just tiny continuous steps will be ok.

When we choose to stay in our comfort zones, we'll find it hard to grow. Stretching your zone will help you to learn and develop. It will enable you to become focused and ambitious. Besides, it will help you to start doing and enjoying things which you never perceived. But why do we gladly stay in our comfort zones even when we know it's painful or not getting us what we want? That's right! It's because of one giant elephant in the room – FEAR.

The Pain of Fear

> *Show me anyone who doesn't experience fear each time they step out of their comfort zone, and I will tell you that they only master their fear.*

If everyone has their comfort zones as I mentioned, that means anyone can experience fear each time they step out of their circle. Right now, you may have had enough of whatever is causing you pain. You have also learned some lessons and have your strength toolbox with you. Likewise, you know what you want; the dream you would like to achieve, but Mr Giant – Fear - is standing in the way.

Mr Fear is stopping you from:

- Speaking up
- Saying no!
- Leaving that painful environment
- Applying for that job
- Taking that college course
- Starting that new relationship
- Ending that abusive relationship
- Losing that weight
- Ending that addiction
- Starting that business
- And many others

As humans, we fear everything in life. As Susan Jeffers rightly puts it,

> *"We fear beginnings; we fear endings; we fear changing; we fear staying stuck; we fear success; we fear failure; we fear living; we fear dying."*

Therefore, imagine that if we're a creature that fears everything in life, how can we thrive? Just as pain is part and parcel of life, fear is also in our DNA! We can't do without it and it is there for our benefit. When we feel fear, it activates our body's defence chemical - adrenaline - which prepares us for either fight or flight. Whichever route we take, whether running away from the situation or confronting it, it has its own immediate, medium, and long-term benefits.

Therefore, the assessment and the decision of fighting or fleeing will be personal. While some might choose to fight, others may decide to flee based on the benefits. My granny used to say, *"Those who always run away from issues will take the issues with them into their graves. But those who confront issues will leave the issues behind and approach their grave like conquerors".* Back then, I didn't understand what she meant even though I always watched her confront her fears head-on, most especially, facing parents whose kids used to bully me in school. However, that still did not give me the audacity to defend myself. I have always fled from issues. But now, I understand that the best way, when possible, is to confront the problem, deal with it, forget about it and focus on the future.

For many of us, we've been told by our inner voices, people, and circumstances to believe that we can't do it. We have been made to think that we are useless and do not deserve to thrive and be happy in life. We've been psychologically confounded in a small circle, and any attempt to push past that circle becomes dreadful. That is why we make ourselves comfortable by using limiting or defeating statements like "I can't", "If only", "But", "I will never" and the like. While we're busy limiting ourselves, others who have mastered their fears are busy **thriving**!

The best way, when possible, is to confront the problem, deal with it, forget about it and focus on the future.

I Chose to Confront the Fear

With my passion for becoming an entrepreneur, I was privileged to be enrolled in a 'Boosting Women in Business' workshop, organised by Staffordshire Chamber of Commerce. This was an opportunity offered to any aspiring female entrepreneur, but many of my *pain pals* declined due to varied reasons. Before enrolling on the course, I was very anxious and fearful about whether I was going to make any positive impact. I had just come out from my emotionally draining relationship, where I had been made to believe that I was a 'useless woman' who had nothing good to offer. I had no voice – well, I had willingly given up my voice and was enjoying my 'yes mentality'. A day before this business workshop, I felt fear and heard the voices saying, "Peggy, you can't run a business...You don't even have the confidence to speak to people. How are you going to market the business and get clients? See, you don't even have the skills and experience. You don't have the money to start any business. Who's going to look after your children? You don't know anyone in this town...You're going to mess up. Why waste your time? I don't think this is the right moment for you ..."

Interestingly, I have a master's degree in management, a degree in law and political science, a level 5 Diploma in leadership and management in health and social care and eight years working experience in health and social care (working with clients suffering from mental health, the elderly, and those with learning disabilities). As if these were not enough, I have my strength toolbox with me from all my years of painful experiences. And was I talking about skills in managing people? For crying out loud, I am a mum to three kids! Curiously, where did all these skills, experiences, and qualifications go? People's biased opinion of me had helped me to flush everything down the drain. I wasn't thinking, talking, and behaving like someone proficient. Nevertheless, I was willing at that moment to do whatever it took to rejuvenate my aspirations and rewrite my story.

When I attended the workshop, I did so not as someone who had all these qualifications and experiences, but as someone who had had enough and wanted to change my life, no matter what! I arrived on time, smartly dressed, walking tall with a friendly smile and looking very confident. By creating a positive impression, other participants were drawn to me. Knowing that I was a bit doubtful of myself, I was always the last to speak because I was mindful not to sabotage myself. I also noticed that they too had their fears to handle. Thus, I wasn't alone! Irrespective of the fact that most participants had the resources to start their businesses, we all had our worries. Gradually, my fear began to fade away and instead of feeling anxious, I started looking forward to attending the course and fully participating.

At the end of the course, I won the top award and was awarded £1000 for my business. That amount may sound insignificant to someone, but that was a 3rd of my operating capital. The best reward for me was that I had turned my Pain of fear into Gain. If you understand the negative impact of low self-esteem and anxiety, (regardless of all the qualifications and experiences we have), you will conclude that we don't achieve or thrive in life, not because we lack the expertise. Instead, it's because we don't feel that we can handle the unknown pain or challenges that lie ahead. Because we think that we can't deal with the pressure of leaving our comfort zones, we embrace the 'comfort-pain zone.' But like I said, the only way to thrive is to master or conquer our fears.

We all manage our fear or anxiety in varied ways. While some may use distracting techniques like counting backwards, focusing on deep breathing, positive imagination or going for a walk, others might use rubber bands, question their thoughts and many more. One helpful technique I used to turn my pain of fear into a gain of calmness was to apply FEAR.

Apply FEAR

F – Feel the Fear
E – Engage in it
A – Accelerate
R – Reassure and Celebrate

Whenever we think of leaving our mental or environmental comfort zones, the depressing feeling of fear kicks in. Fear will always knock on your door, and you need to get used to it because it's a recurrent visitor. It – will – always – come! The best you can do is to open the door and welcome the fear. So, you will still feel fear.

F- Feel the Fear

This is what happened to me the first time I was invited to speak to a room full of businesswomen. It was my first time of public speaking and sharing my story of Pain to Gain to motivate others in the room. Although I had prepared my content, the rush of adrenaline was intense each time

I pictured myself in the room. I went pale within a few days because I lost my appetite. Again, the voices couldn't stop tormenting me. "You're going to mess up...No one is going to take you seriously... Give it up ..." I felt so much fear that I almost declined the invitation. But I applied

E – Engaged in it.

Like I said, fear is a visitor and, whether we welcome it or pretend as if it doesn't exist, determines the quality of our relationship with fear. In my case, I chose to embrace the fear and we engaged in a dialogue. I needed a conversation to interrogate or question its purpose for visiting. Equally, it was necessary to let it know that **"this is my house, and I have the authority to choose who comes in and what they say"**. In my head, whispering to myself, I started my questioning session. I said,

*"Ok, Fear, I must admit I can feel you, but I don't know your problem. Yes, I know this is my first time public speaking, but I already know what I want to say! I wrote it myself, and I am comfortable with the content. I am not going to mess up, and even if I did, everyone makes mistakes, and it will also be a learning curve for me. Even if no one takes me seriously, I will still be proud that I stepped out and delivered my message. By the way, I am looking forward to it, and there is **nothing** you can do to stop me. So, **Leave My House Right Now!**"*

After a dialogue, it is important that we should immediately engage in action – step out and do whatever you need to start the change process. As soon as I finished interrogating my fear of public speaking, I hit the computer and sent a confirmation message to the event coordinator, pledging my 100% attendance. So, for you, it might be the fear of enrolling on that course, speaking up, starting that relationship, seeking professional help, etc. Whatever it is, just do it!

I must mention that there is a category of fear that is very stubborn – they'll always show their ugly heads at 'your door' even after chasing them. Fear of public speaking is one of them. As the event was drawing closer, the pressure started mounting again. I could feel the stiffness, butterfly feeling, and banging headache. The voices dared me again, "… I told you, you shouldn't have. You can't handle it. You'll mess up…" But at this point, I applied,

A – Accelerate!

I told the fear that, *"there was no backing or slowing down. I still desire to speak at that event, and I will do whatever it takes to show up and speak!"* I accelerated my efforts to keep me calm and prepared. I went to the gym, I presented in front of my kids, performed in front of my *pain pals*, practised over and over in front of the mirror, and I did all I could to distract myself from thinking about the event. If this applies to you and you still want to achieve that dream, doubling your efforts to deal with any barrier becomes crucial. On the other hand, increasing your efforts can also be quite overwhelming and painful, especially If you're doing something new to you. For me, I felt exhausted at one point, trying to get everything right, but then I applied,

R – Reassure and celebrate.

Reassurance begins with our inner authoritative voice. I patted myself and said, *"Well done! You're doing very well.*

You're incredible! You need to take it one step at a time, and a day at a time. This is your passion, and I know you can handle it." Each time I repeated these sentences, I felt energised and motivated. I also approached friends and families who believed in my passion and they boosted me. Besides, I celebrated my micro wins with myself and my kids. I knew I had come too far and the more I praised my efforts, the more I wanted to do more.

When the day finally came, I nailed it! The audience couldn't believe it was my first-time public speaking – looking smart, no notes, excellent composure and audience connection. After my presentation, I was the 'star' of the event; people approaching me to congratulate and thank me for inspiring them. Some came for a hug and a handshake, and others came for my business card – of which, unfortunately, I had none! So yes! I was empowered! My self-confidence soared and I turned my Pain of public speaking into Gain. As *Pain Candidates,* irrespective of your aspirations, once you can master your fear, your journey to thriving or bouncing back to life will be easier than you think. As discussed in the next chapter, accepting and conquering our fears facilitates accepting responsibility for our lives. Hang on! Did I say, "accepting responsibility for our lives"? This is definitely the sentence that escaped my memory. By the way, why did I have to accept responsibility when others hurt me? It was not my fault!

> **We don't achieve or thrive in life, not because**
> **we lack the expertise. Instead, it's because we**
> **don't feel that we can handle the unknown**
> **pain or challenges that lie ahead.**

CHAPTER 4

Step 2 – Accept Responsibility

Accepting responsibility gives you the brush and the dustpan; you can easily clean up the mess.

Imagine sitting relaxed in your cleaned, well-organised living room and watching your favourite TV programme. Suddenly, you get a knock on the door and it's a surprise visit from a friend. Apparently, this friend is usually very untidy, yet you usher him in and offer him some tea and biscuits. In the process of eating, he messes the sofa and your carpet and doesn't bother to clean it up. On your part, you become angry about it and demand him to clean up, which he refuses and walks off. Would you clean up the mess or continue waiting for him to come and clean it?

In this journey called life, people and events will cross our paths. Some could be good, others bad and some, very nasty. Many will invade our lives, mess it up and leave. And the choice is ours whether to clean the mess or sit on it. If there is one truth I hold dearly, after all my painful experiences in life, it is to take 100% responsibility for my life. That means, accept 100% responsibility for my past, present and my future.

The day I revealed this to my *pain pals*, during a coffee meeting, I was almost thrown out of the room. In fact, I was looked upon as insane. One invaded my private space, looked at me sternly and said, "Well, that's your opinion". Another angrily yelled, "Are you mad to tell me to accept responsibility? I am in this pain because my partner abused me. He destroyed my life, took away my dreams. He controlled all my money and left me penniless…" Yet, another gave me the F-word and said, "I can never accept responsibility for what my family did to me." And to be honest with you, I could feel their anguish and what they meant when they blamed their partners, families, friends and events for the miseries in their lives. No one deserves to be treated like trash and that is the reason why I am passionate about what I do: Inspiring especially survivors of modern slavery, childhood, and domestic abuse to unlock their passions and potentials, take back control of their lives and thrive. When we know our worth, we won't allow people to take away our value.

Interestingly, we live in a 'Blame Game' society, where it is reasonable and acceptable to blame people, things or events for the mishaps in life. Consciously or unconsciously, we feel compelled to justify and distance ourselves from any action that exposes our weaknesses. We see these daily:

- Why are you late for work? Because I was stuck in traffic. So, traffic is blamed.

- Why did you lose your job? Because my boss didn't like me. The boss is blamed.
- Why did your relationship break up? Because my partner caused it. Partner is blamed.
- Why don't you cook healthy food? Because my mum didn't teach me how to cook. Mum is blamed.
- Why are you overweight? Because I am stressed. Stress is blamed.
- Why didn't you complete that project? Because there was no time. Time is blamed.
- Why did you wake up late? Because my alarm didn't go off. The clock is blamed.

It is worth mentioning that, as *Pain Candidates*, when we were minors (0-16 or 17 years), we had no power or control over those that inflicted mental or physical pain on us. In my case, cited in Chapter One, I couldn't stop the traditional doctor from inflicting pain on me or my schoolmates bullying me; neither could Meg stop her father from raping her. We were vulnerable and at the mercy of those whom we trusted, but sadly, they turned and abused us. Once we became adults, we had our mental capacity, which empowered us to make decisions without interference. We could confront people and say, "Enough!" By choice, we could choose and follow our future direction. Aren't we lucky?

Many will invade our lives, mess it up and leave. And the choice is ours whether to clean the mess or sit on it.

Choice: Our Human Right

Choice is an act of selecting between two or more options. Although each day presents us with the need to exercise our human rights to choose, most people neglect the rights. We often settle with choices that leave us devastated, frustrated and in pain. Nevertheless, it is essential to mention that sometimes our options place us in a dilemma where all choices would end in pain. That can be likened to choosing between 'the deep sea and a burning furnace", but the most valuable thing is that we must make a choice! If I tell you that what you're experiencing now, or whatever painful experiences you faced as an adult is your choice, how would that sound? That may sound rude or unempathetic, but is it? When I reflected over my ability as an adult to choose, I concluded that:

- I had the choice to be assertive and voice my feelings, but I didn't.
- I had the choice to leave my relationship, yet I stayed until I was physically and emotionally exhausted.
- I had the choice to manage my emotions, yet I allowed them to control me.
- I had the choice to learn and grow, but I chose to remain in my comfort zone.
- I had the choice to ditch all my negative and unhelpful friends, but I didn't.
- I had the choice to manage my finances and save more, yet I did not.
- I had the choice to seek help, but I didn't.

We all have a reason for our actions and omission or for being in our current position. However, if we are honest with ourselves, we should take responsibility. If we honestly want to leave our mental or physical comfort zones, we will. Only you can stop yourself. I love Demon Wayans' quote which says, *"Nobody can stop you but you. And shame on you if you're the one who stops yourself"*. This is one of the quotes that got me stirred to rescue myself. Usually, the conditions might not be favourable; fear will strike us and oppression will deter us. However, if we chose to accelerate, we could. And, yes! You can do this because you are your saving grace and the only person responsible for your life. Personally, if there is anyone I need to blame, it should be me! Nevertheless, I say that from the standpoint of strength and empowerment. This positivity gives me the zeal to take back control of every area of my life. I choose to be happy and the responsibility lies on me. After all, it's my life! At least I know that I have the brush and the dustpan, and I can easily clean up any mess, rather than wait for someone or something else to do it for me. What have you chosen, and what would you do to make it a reality?

**I choose to be happy and the responsibility
lies on me.**

The Pain of Blame Game

My body scars, the death of my best friend and granny, the emotional trauma and rejection in my relationships constantly recalled how events unfolded. Before my *mental rebirth*,[4] I blamed my parents for not being there for me when I needed them. I blamed the medical doctors for not diagnosing my heart disease early enough. I also blamed the traditional doctors for their abominable treatment. Moreover, I blamed the community for not saving my friend's life, blamed the medical doctors for not saving my granny's life and blamed my partner for the emotional abuse. I spent my whole time blaming people and events for my painful experiences, but that did not change anything. Instead, it added more pain because it generated negative emotions (anger, grief, sadness, guilt, revenge, frustration and depression), which left me miserable and made me dislike others.

When I embarked on my journey to recovery, the mindset I cultivated was that of **Gain**. Although I may feel resentful of these painful occurrences, the experiences helped to define who I am today because they empowered my development of strength and courage. I am sure you're familiar with the saying, *"what doesn't kill you, only makes you stronger"*. That's right! I wanted to see through the lenses of a survivor, and not a victim. Thanks to all my painful experiences, I can now appreciate and value life. Life is too short for any second to be wasted on negative blaming. Now, I understand what it means to sacrifice for a loved one, the same way my granny did for me. I don't easily give up on people, especially my loved ones. I appreciate and celebrate friendship because

---

[4] Mental Rebirth refers to my mental conditioning before my recovery journey

anything could happen at any time. My advocacy against obnoxious practices, especially on children, is thanks to the pain I went through. My abilities to set boundaries in my relationships and to communicate assertively are also thanks to my pain. When I look at my scars, I see heroism, and choosing to turn my pain into gain has brought out the best in me. What do you see? Do the emotional and physical scars serve as a source of your strength? Choosing to see heroism in the scars you bear can be a turning point in your life.

> **Life is too short for any second to be wasted on negative blaming.**

It Doesn't Mean You are Weak

As *Pain Candidates*, the phrase 'accept responsibility' is usually misconstrued to mean being guilty, to be blamed, being weak or being overburdened – but that's not true. Many victim-survivors feel intimidated by the phrase. For some, it makes them vulnerable and less empowered, which is far from the truth. In my view, accepting responsibility comes in two dimensions:

1. Accepting responsibility for our thoughts, emotions, words and behaviours.
2. Accepting responsibility for whatever happened or is happening in our lives as adults.

For the former, accepting responsibility means not blaming someone for the thoughts we allowed in our minds, especially if they were harmful. Secondly, not blaming someone for the emotions we generated, especially if they were negative. And lastly, not blaming someone for the words we expressed and the behaviours we exhibited, especially if they were harmful. We create our universe with our thoughts, emotions, words and actions.

Maggie, one of my *pain pals*, had a row at work following constant pressure from her supervisor. In the process, she became furious, insulted her boss and walked out of the office. Because of her poor conduct, she was sacked. Still, she refused to accept responsibility for her behaviour and blamed her boss for pushing her to her limit. Maggie believed she was sacked because her boss never liked her, and I couldn't tell if her assertion was correct. However, Maggie needed to accept responsibility for her actions. She needed to understand that, irrespective of her boss' intention or pressure, she had the choice to act differently. Learning to accept responsibility for her poor behaviour would prevent a similar outcome. Amusingly, the negative thought she conceived came from her mind, not from her boss. Maggie's thoughts generated her negative emotions, which resulted in offensive words and ultimately, her action to impulsively leave the office. Maggie finally agreed with me as she testified that her colleague, who was also put under similar pressure, was promoted and she loved her job! This colleague chose to take the Pain of pressure as a Gain to growth. So, I asked Maggie, "Who was the problem, you or your boss?" And with a guilty smile, she said, "Me." Therefore, it is usually easy to blame people or events for the pain in our lives. Meanwhile, we should be acknowledging the fact that we have the choice to think, talk and behave in ways that will work in our favour.

Accepting responsibility for our thoughts, words and actions doesn't mean we are weak or guilty. It simply means we acknowledge the fact that we are human, we have weaknesses and make mistakes. Until we recognise and address those weaknesses, we might continue to go through the same cycle of mistakes. Maggie needed to accept that some of her weaknesses were finding it difficult working under pressure, lack of patience and poor anger management – which is okay! It was crucial to accept responsibility for her weaknesses and improve upon them, which her employer would have been willing to help with, had she mentioned it. If we admit that we have weaknesses, we will also learn not to overreact to the actions or omissions of others. Besides, we would cultivate a habit of accepting people for who and what they are. We would also be judging people's intentions instead of their behaviours and learning to see the best version of them.

The fact that we have weaknesses doesn't make us inadequate. Hence, we don't need to punish ourselves and others for acting unsatisfactorily. Do not feel like you are stupid, or you are never going to change or will always be making mistakes. When events present themselves before us, we usually act in the best way we can. Although the result may be positive or negative, we remain confident because we know we have done our best to manage the situation. Also, whatever the outcome, we shouldn't be too hard on ourselves and others – after all, we are just human, with weaknesses and we are prone to mistakes!

As we will discuss in Chapter Six, accepting responsibility also means accepting and taking control of our thought patterns. We need to be conscious of the voices that seem to control our behaviours. When we accept responsibility for our inner voices, we command power and control over our thoughts. Likewise, we can choose the direction of our thoughts to align with our values and our purpose.

Accepting responsibility for our thoughts, words and actions doesn't mean we are weak or guilty. It simply means, we acknowledge the fact that we are human, we have weaknesses and make mistakes.

The second dimension of accepting responsibility is to accept responsibility for the past and current happenings in our lives as adults. Remember, I mentioned that once we become adults, we have the choice to choose whether to accept people's nasty behaviours or stand up to them and say, "Enough"! We have the choice to seek help or stay silent. We also have the choice to use challenges in our lives to create opportunities for ourselves or to remain as victims. If we decide to let people or events treat us miserably, there will be no need for apportioning blame. This is because we had the choice to stop them or create opportunities for ourselves, but we didn't.

When I finally had another conversation with Linda, (the *pain pal* in Chapter Two who demanded to know my secret to recovery), she blamed her ex-partner for her poor financial status, anxiety, low self-esteem and pessimism. And honestly,

I could feel her bitterness and frustration; a tortuous feeling that nobody deserves. Then she turned and asked me, "Peggy, do you feel the same?" Sincerely, when I left my relationship, I felt and thought the same as her. However, when I chose to embark on my *mental rebirth* journey, my mindset changed. "I felt the same before, but not now," I responded to Linda. "Then how did you do it?" she asked again.

It Takes Two to Tango

I am sure you've heard the phrase, "It takes two to tango." Relationship crisis, which tops the charts for pain in our lives, usually involves two or more parties. Whenever something goes wrong, each party would have contributed in one way or the other. As cited earlier, we typically do not openly accept our faults. Even when fully aware of the impact of our behaviours towards the relationship breakup, we still become evasive. We continue to declare ourselves righteous to evade responsibility, and by so doing, we fail to realise that we are laying grounds for our devastation and pain.

When I left my relationship, the blame game was never-ending. My partner and I were throwing 'blame blows' back and forth, which wasn't helping anyone. It was draining all of the energy out of me because pushing blame also involves trying to defend ourselves as not being the guilty one. It is exhausting! As a result, I decided that the best way I could save my time and energy was to work on myself (mental rebirth). For me, it wasn't about my partner anymore, but about me! I wanted to change myself. I read self-help books and attended training workshops to change myself. In that process, I made a vow to myself that no matter what, I wouldn't waste a second pointing a finger at anyone for the misery in my life. I took 100% responsibility for whatever happened in my life. After all, I had the choice to speak up or set healthy boundaries, yet I didn't. I was even perceived as a 'weak woman' who couldn't stand up for herself. In other words, I gave my power away and became vulnerable. Thus, if anything, I wasn't going to accept responsibility for people's behaviour, but take responsibility for having allowed others to inflict pain on me. Remember, this journey is not about your partner, friend, mum, dad or your boss; it is about you. You want to change your life, and it is up to these people to go change their own lives.

Changing me required me to identify all my areas of weakness and develop ways to improve them. Some of my weaknesses included passiveness, people-pleasing, impulsiveness, poor communication, poor budgeting skills, inconsistency, inflexibility, lack of purpose and low self-esteem. Interestingly, my upbringing and mental conditioning also contributed to me being or acting this way. Notwithstanding, now, as an adult, I have the choice to recondition and retrain my mind to my gain. So, each day, I focused on improving my weaknesses. Today, I communicate more assertively, I am more conscientious, I have a purposeful life, a quality relationship with myself, and a passion for changing lives. If I hadn't taken 100% responsibility for my life, you wouldn't have been reading this book. I turned my Blames into Gain and my weaknesses into strengths. I also moved from barely surviving psychologically, physically, financially, spiritually, socially and professionally, to thriving in all these areas within a short period. That's the magic of taking responsibility for one's life.

Each time we blame others, we don't only create negative energy, we also distance ourselves from the solution. In other words, we are saying, "We did nothing wrong and, therefore, have nothing to change about us or the event." We fail to comprehend that each time we do that, we stifle our growth. I don't call my mistakes, 'mistakes', I call them, 'lessons'. Even if I make 100 mistakes, I prefer to say, I learned 100 lessons. This enables me to see my mistakes as gains. It helps me to learn and grow and not to feel ashamed to accept responsibility for my 'lessons'. Those who accept responsibility for their lives take back control of every area of their lives. They control their emotions, health, finances, careers, kids' wellbeing, relationship - and the list goes on. This is because if we admit that we messed up somewhere, we can also clean up the mess quickly. But as aforementioned, pushing blame is like asking or waiting for someone else to clean up the mess for you, and you could wait forever! Taking responsibility for our lives also means accepting adverse events as an opportunity or gateway for our growth and flourishing. A pain presented before you may be your 'Saving Grace' if you choose to see it with the lenses of gain. My relationship breakup was a gateway to finding and living my purpose, which I enjoy because of the lives I transform each day. We don't have to depend on people or events for our success or happiness. Unfortunately, those who push blame are likely to keep repeating the same painful behaviour and expecting others or circumstances to change. These are the kind of people who, sadly, could change their partners, jobs or friends, yet replicate the same behaviour, while expecting a different result. As Albert Einstein said, **"Insanity is doing the same thing, over and over again, but expecting different results."** I must admit that embarking on such a journey doesn't happen overnight. It takes time, patience and commitment. It involves leaving the past behind and focusing on you. It doesn't matter if people are still blaming or labelling you; it won't change anything. Do you choose to stay in that box of public opinion, or do you prefer to break free and be who you were born to be?

Those who push blame are likely to keep repeating the same painful behaviour but expecting others or circumstances to change.

The Pain of a Victim Mindset

Which statement is more empowering? Is it, "I am a victim" or "I am a survivor?"

In my view, when we're caught up in the pain environment or event and can't escape it, it can be ok to label oneself as a victim. This is because, at that moment, you don't know if you would be able or lucky enough to escape or survive from the trauma. However, once you have braved it, sought help and leave the environment or get healed, you become a survivor. As *Pain Candidates*, it may take longer to recover emotionally or physically, but having a courageous mindset can speed up our recovery. Each time I say, "I am a survivor or a fighter", it enhances my mental resilience and raises my hopes for a lasting recovery. Having survived my pain, I dislike the term *victim* because it labels me as a "loser", "sufferer" or "prey". As much as I despise the word, I don't like talking and acting like a victim.

I have noticed that we like to engrave the word *victim* on our foreheads. Just by looking at us or hearing us speak, one can tell that we're victims of such and such. For some reason, we love to make people sympathise with us. Don't get me wrong. I understand that it is consoling when people empathise with us. This is especially when we are going through challenging moments like a health crisis, bereavement, job loss, relationship breakup and others. My only problem is that we may tend to adhere to the negatives of the pain while negating the positives (lessons learned, or strength developed). There is nothing wrong in sharing your pain with someone from the standpoint of strength. For example, "Although I wasn't happy that I was sacked from my job, I have also learned a lesson to manage my emotions and treat people fairly." By releasing positive energy, it gives us hope and the ability to heal faster. But then, if all we think and talk about is 'negative, pity and victim,' that also hampers our healing.

As we'll be discussing in the next chapter, you have a hidden treasure of energy within you which is enough to keep you alight. In addition, our passion, which becomes our purpose in life, is derived from our pain. All along, I was carrying a treasure within me, which I didn't realise until my breaking point. That treasure has become my purpose or motive for life, which makes me believe in Charles Swindoll's statement;

"I am convinced that life is 10% what happens to me and 90% how I react to it." In other words, let our Pain be 10% and our Gain be 90%.

CHAPTER 5

Step 3 – Motive Or Purpose In Life

*"The two most important days in your life are the
day you are born and the day you find out why."*
– Mark Twain

My little son walked up to me one evening after watching a
Youtuber and asked me, "Mum, what's a purpose?" "It is the
reason for doing something", I responded. "Can something or
someone be created for a purpose?" "Yes, games are created
for a motive or purpose – for entertainment, learning and
creativity, and everything and everyone was created for a
motive or purpose too. Why do you ask?" I inquired. And
he said, "Because my favourite YouTuber said gaming is his
purpose for living… I love gaming too; does that mean it's
also my purpose for living?"

Modern-day video games have become a household
necessity and some kids can't do without them. Due to its
addictive nature, some kids, like my son, might believe that
gaming is their life's purpose, which isn't. Regarding my son's
question, it is too early to tell if gaming is his purpose for life,

but he has a life's purpose, just as we all do. Think about the dreams you expressed when you were a child and what you wanted when you become an adult. Have you achieved those dreams? Maybe you grew up and realised that it wasn't really what you wanted and so you ditched it. What about the ones you wished for as teenagers or adults? Maybe you're multi-talented and have different aspirations such that you can't determine which of them is your purpose. Again, perhaps the traumatic events in your life have choked your dreams or purpose in life. Being in such a dilemma can be painful! Hence, it is my hope that this chapter will help you to find your purpose in life – the reason why you were born.

Why were you born?

You would be surprised with the answers you get from friends and family when asked this question. You could get responses like:

- I don't know!
- My parents said I was born so they could claim some financial support.
- My parents said my birth wasn't planned; I was born by mistake.
- I was born to be abused and used by others.
- I was born because my parents needed a child.

Irrespective of the response you have, one thing I am confident of is that each of us was born for a unique and valuable purpose. Everyone has something to offer to another in life. This purpose is something unique to you that no other person has and is hidden within you. Each of us is a vessel carrying a unique solution, and someone has a problem which requires your solution as well as mine. Until we provide that solution, life may seem incomplete for us and to the beneficiaries of our unique purposes. Have you ever gotten to a point where you feel like something is missing in your life? I mean that point where, despite the successes in your family life, finances, health and career, you keep asking, "Is this all there is to life?" Our journey from Pain to Gain also means finding and living our purpose in life.

In my view, one's purpose in life is that innate passion which is accompanied by unique skills and abilities to meet a need in the world around you. It is something that we enjoy doing and which may come to us effortlessly – that service which, when delivered, produces an internal satisfaction which money cannot buy. It is also what makes us get up in the morning, and without which our lives will be meaningless. We all have skills, abilities and natural gifts given to us to meet a need in our communities and the world at large. At times, we can devalue these talents or we might not even be aware that they are unique to us.

During my *mental rebirth,* after researching about our purposes in life, I realised that my purpose is my passion, and my passion is writing, motivating, caring for the elderly, cooking, dancing, cleaning, and singing. These are activities that I enjoy doing any day and anytime. What is that activity that brings joy into your life and the lives of those around you? You may be a chef, teacher, medical professional, builder, cleaner, accountant, designer, manager and the like, but the most crucial question is, do you love and enjoy what you do? Were you persuaded by someone or circumstances to do

what you do, or did you follow your heart? Do you feel you
were born for it? With the advent and the impact of Covid-19,
answering these questions may be challenging. Nevertheless,
Covid-19 has also awoken hidden skills and opportunities.

> **Each of us is a vessel carrying a unique
> solution, and someone has a problem which
> requires your solution. Until we provide that
> solution, life may seem incomplete for us and
> to the beneficiaries of our unique purposes.**

Our unique purposes possess abilities, skills, and talents
that we can tap into to change our lives and those of others.
Surprisingly, these qualities may be underutilised or lying
dormant within us. We might occupy ourselves pursuing
goals and vocations which do not bring us fulfilment and
meaning in life. Sometimes, situations may lead us to engage
in activities that are contrary to our passion. At other times,
other circumstances may help to bring us to the discovery
of our unique purposes. As you will come to realise, mine
was prompted by the latter. As *Pain Candidates*, we usually
doubt our abilities and potential to turn our pain into gain.
Remember that in Chapter Two, I argued that our personal
strengths are the tools that we use to confront our challenges.
This means that we should never underestimate our personal
strengths and the lessons learned in life. We need to be
proud of who, and what we are. That's right! We must be
proud of our capabilities and use them to our advantage. My
passion for writing, which I developed during my childhood
rejection, has become my most significant therapy – I call

it my "antidepressant" because it takes my mind off painful memories, keeps me calm and gives me a meaning in life.

Our personal strengths are the tools that we use to confront our challenges.

Are You Settling for Less in Life?

You might have read the preceding paragraphs and are nodding your head because you feel that you're not pursuing your passion. Or you've been unable to reach your higher needs of esteem and self-actualisation as stated in Maslow's hierarchy of needs. You may even be feeling some sense of frustration or regret. But let me reassure you that as a *Pain Candidate*, you're not alone. During my *mental rebirth*, one thing that got me thinking was Maslow's hierarchy of needs as seen below.

Maslow's hierarchy of needs is a motivational theory in psychology which has five levels of human needs. These needs are arranged in a hierarchical order, from bottom to top. The needs at the bottom would usually be satisfied before an individual reached for the higher needs. The physiological, safety, belonging and love, and esteem needs are known as deficiency needs. That means, we longed for these needs because of deprivation, and once these needs are satisfied, our hunger for it decreases. When we're hungry, for example, we need food. Once we eat, our hunger decreases or fades away. The self-actualisation needs (which are the highest needs), are called growth needs, which means we pursue these needs because of our desire for personal growth. When these growth needs are reasonably satisfied, we may reach our highest level of self-actualisation or full potential.

Thus, looking at this hierarchy of needs, it occurred to me that I was settling for less in life. I had food, clothes, shelter, rest, safety, and relationships, but I struggled with self-esteem, felt unfulfilled and wasn't achieving my full potential. I also realised that our painful experiences have a negative impact on our needs, especially our highest need of self-actualisation. As a *Pain Candidate*, I was hungry for personal growth, and as Maslow states, "to become everything one is capable of becoming" (Maslow, 1987, p.64). I would add that reaching our full potential could be that point where we turn our pain into passion; our passion becomes our purpose, and our purpose creates the desire to become the best that we can be.

Interestingly, when our highest need is met, our motivation for personal development increases. It's like the more we learn, the more we want to learn – and it's such a fantastic experience! However, it can also be frustrating to know that pain can hinder our potentials. From the perspective of a *Pain Candidate*, we would usually, due to various traumas in our lives, settle for the lower needs. When I left my relationship and became homeless, all I was interested in was a roof over our heads. I wasn't bothered about self-esteem, career or life purpose. In some cases, painful events in our lives may cause us to fluctuate between these needs. For example, you could have an intimate partner today, and become lonely the next day. Or you could have a comfortable home today and become homeless the next day. No matter what pain you have experienced or are experiencing right now, I must admit that any painful event can affect our needs. It can prevent us from reaching our highest potentials, except we choose to use that pain to our benefit. We also need to be willing to seek personal growth and go for the higher needs in life, which, in turn, enhances the quality of our fundamental or lower needs. Remember the Pain Heroes I cited in Chapter Two – Oprah and others? Reaching their highest potentials have enhanced their lower needs; they have their dream homes, eat the best food, have the safety required, have meaningful relationships, have higher self-esteem and are highly respected for their achievements. And guess what? This is not reserved for specific people; you and I can also reach our full potential. The only question is, "Are we willing?"

Which Zone are You?

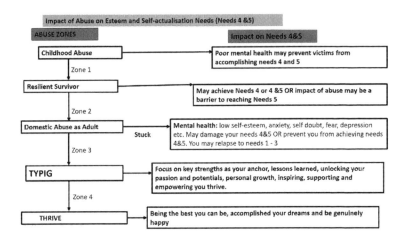

I would like to share with you this illustration which I use in my training course - Turning Your Pain into Gain (TYPIG). It helps me to demonstrate to participants the impact of childhood or domestic abuse on our highest needs of esteem and self-actualisation – which I refer to as needs 4 & 5. Using my childhood experiences, as shared with you in Chapter One, and relating it to how it affected my highest needs, I couldn't help but ponder on how our dreams and purpose in life can be damaged by pain. For anyone who has experienced childhood abuse or domestic abuse, the illustration above summarises the impact it has on our needs.

Zone one is where a child experiences abuse. Like me, you might have had the bottom needs like food, water, shelter, clothes and rest. Others may have had security, stability, safety and protection by loved ones. We could also have been loved by our family and friends, which created the feeling of belonging. Nevertheless, the unfolding of events may have left us vulnerable and abused by members of our family, friends, trusted institutions, strangers and the community. The psychological or physical impact of the abuse could affect our mental and physical growth and development. Mentally, we may be left with challenges like low self-esteem, fear, anxiety, self-doubt, depression, sleeplessness, guilt and shame, poor decision-making abilities, etc. And sadly, due to the lack of professional intervention, we may carry these challenges into adulthood.

As adults, events may trigger our painful memories, which could also affect our daily functioning. As you will read in subsequent chapters, this may continue to create negative emotions and behaviours which affect our mental and physical wellbeing. Many *Pain Candidates* have found themselves in positions where the effects of abuse caused them to drop out of school. Some engaged in addictive behaviours as coping strategies leading them to become more susceptible to further abuse. Besides, many *Pain Candidates* do not have the chance or the courage and ability to embrace opportunities that would enable them to reach their needs of esteem and self-actualisation. To achieve esteem needs, Maslow indicates that through our accomplishments, we can develop self-respect and gain respect from others. For *Pain Candidates*, this might not be easy because we usually struggle with our self-worth and the courage to demand respect from others. This is partly because most survivors of abuse can experience passiveness, low self-esteem and anxiety based on our limiting beliefs, and these also limit others' respect towards us. For example, each time you tell yourself that "I'm a failure or stupid", that's exactly what others begin to think of you, hence, disrespecting you. Similarly, because we doubt our inner abilities, we may struggle to reach our full potentials.

Zone two is for resilient survivors, those *Pain Candidates* like me who, despite our childhood abuse, braved the odds and hung onto optimism to achieve our esteem needs. For others, they might have been encouraged by their loved ones to seek professional help and achieve their aspirations. Although I didn't get any professional help as a child, I was determined to be educated and held varied career roles which gave me a sense of accomplishment. Though I doubted myself and my abilities, I was highly revered by my clients and my colleagues. However, the impact of childhood abuse remained a barrier to reaching my highest potential.

Zone three is where adult domestic abuse may occur. According to the Office for National Statistics for England and Wales, 51% of adults who experienced childhood abuse also suffer domestic violence in later life. Although the reasons for this could vary, it usually narrows down to causes like low self-esteem, passiveness, anxiety, self-doubt, inherited limiting beliefs, depression and addictive behaviours, to name a few. As aforementioned, when we experience abuse in adulthood, it might further damage our cognitive abilities, leaving us with fear and self-doubt. It also limits our capabilities to reach self-fulfilment. Domestic abuse could affect every part of our lives – job, relationships, children, social life, finances, behaviour, emotional and physical health and the like. Besides this, it causes victims to lose their higher needs (esteem and self-actualisation) or may prevent them from fulfilling these needs. This is the point where we might lose our jobs, money, home, kids, independence, businesses, reputation, motivation... and the list goes on. Unfortunately, we could even relapse, struggling to meet lower needs like food, shelter, clothes, safety, love and belonging. Sadly enough, even after meeting our basic needs, the experience might decapitate our motivation and leaving us stuck in this zone. We might continue settling for less because we doubt our inner strength and abilities to bounce back to life.

Whether you belong to zones one, two or three, the good news is that **zone four** is where turning your pain into gain (TYPIG) comes in. As already mentioned, this is when we focus on our core strengths, using the lessons learned to our advantage, and when we unlock our passions and potentials and re-ignite our willingness for personal growth. As said,

> **It is that point where we turn our pain into passions, our passions become our purpose, and our purpose creates the desire to become the best that we can be, which enables us to live a thriving life.**

Finding our life purpose can be a daunting task, especially after passing through painful experiences. This is because these experiences damage our mindsets and self-confidence and paralyse us with fear. Thus, we typically fear the discomfort of facing our truth even if it's for good. Interestingly, while others are fortunate to find and live their purpose early on in life, others find theirs at a later stage in life and some never get to find theirs. My intention in writing this book is to guide those who, like me, have been battling with their real purpose in life, doubting their abilities, burdened with fear, outweighed by societal norms, and under the yoke of abuse which destroyed their self-image. It is written for you who think they will never find their purpose in life. It is to inspire you to begin working on achieving your dreams because it is never too late. You deserve to reach your full potential and enjoy life to the fullest.

Which category do you belong to?

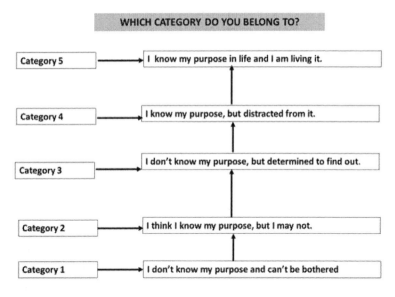

When it comes to knowing our purpose in life, based on my experience, I would say there are five categories of people. The first and lowest category defines those who do not know their purpose and have deliberately chosen not to know. The second category is for those who think they know their purpose, yet when asked, they get confused because they do not know their purposes and having an illusion of life. The third category is those who do not know their purpose at all but are determined to find out. The fourth category is those who know their purpose yet are distracted from it. And the final and highest category is those who know their purpose in life and are living it. We aim to get to the 5th category because that's where we thrive in life.

The most painful categories are the 2nd and 4th. Those who think they know their purpose but they don't are the type that always follow the crowd or do something for different motives than passion. On the other hand, those who know their purpose and yet are distracted from it might end life feeling regret and being angry with themselves. This is because they had the keys to the door of happiness and refused to open the door. It is fair to say that we might, at some point in our lives, go through all five categories before finally finding and living our purpose.

Category 1

It is common to begin by not knowing our purpose in life and not being bothered about it. After all, we could say we have our necessities (food, clothes, and shelter) in life, and we are happy! As no one bothers when satisfied, so too, we may not be bothered to utilise our gifts or learn new skills to benefit ourselves and others. Before my turning point, as mentioned at the start of this book, I fitted into this category. After briefly becoming homeless, I was glad that we had shelter, food, clothes and some stability. Still, I was so worried about our future and the thoughts of my experiences were emotionally draining. I unconsciously developed an unhealthy routine – drop kids in school, come back home, cry, prepare their meal, return to my weeping, pick them from school, spend some time with them and off to bed. I couldn't be bothered to know my purpose in life. In the same light, many who experience pain or have been forced by their circumstances to lose focus fall into this category. We would usually be satisfied with our lifestyles and not be bothered to reach our highest potentials. However, as our need to belong, engage and be financially secure increases, we then shift to category two.

Category 2

This is where we get into a vocation, not because we love it, but because we want remuneration, bonuses, status, some sense of belonging and to satisfy family, public opinion, or statutory requirement. When I reflect on this category, it recalls the time when I left my health care job for a payroll job. As you will read later, even though I enjoyed my job, I was humiliated by working as a health care assistant. In order to respect public opinion, I trained and got an office job as a payroll assistant. Although I worked 9-5 and had weekends for myself and family, I disliked the job – I didn't like the work environment. In the beginning, I enjoyed the job environment and my responsibilities, however, as time went on, my desire and commitment began to depreciate. Many of us within this category would dread waking on the next day and would look for any viable reason to call off work because there is no passion in what we do. We might be physically present at work, but emotionally absent because we're no longer interested in the job. We can even feel trapped and unskilled in our careers. As mentioned above, this is that point where, despite the successes in your family life, finances, career, social network and the like, you keep asking, "Is this all there is to life?" The need for filling that vacuum or emptiness in our lives may ignite our search for our purpose. This is when we get to category three.

Category 3

This is the category where we ignite our consciousness or wake up to the fact that enough is enough. After I reached my breaking point, I was determined to transform my life. We could develop the desire to learn and know by reading books, attending training sessions, listening to others' stories, re-evaluating our goals, evaluating our life wheels, practising mindfulness, seeking professional guidance, changing our mindset, and eliminating limiting beliefs, taking responsibility for our lives, creating healthy habits and many more. This category can sometimes be confusing and burdened with so much information. People like me, who have many passions in life, may find it difficult to conclude what they want to accept as their purpose in life. In my experience, I was grappling between creating a domiciliary care company or pursuing my passion for writing, speaking and coaching. Going through this can be emotionally painful, and this uncertainty might lead us to category four.

Category 4

This is where we can know our purpose yet get distracted from it. We may want to quit our job and gain employment with a company that delivers the services that aligned with our passion or purpose. We could also want to create our own business and use our skills and abilities to change lives, thereby living a purposeful life. We might even want to volunteer our time, energy, skills and resources for good causes. Yet, we might also become distracted by fear of the unknown and start to doubt our abilities. Our comfort zones, limiting beliefs, lack of self-confidence, financial and family responsibilities, and friends' scepticism can also distract us from living our purpose. If you're in this category, I would suggest you do what I did: seeking professional guidance, developing yourself and listening to your intuition can help you to find the right direction. It is my wish that by the time you finish reading this book, you would have learned some tools and techniques which will aid you to pursue whichever purpose-driven path you may like to take. When you do, it will move you to the highest category.

Category 5

The final category is when we know our purpose, develop and live it. This category is when we feel alive in ourselves and are always looking forward to doing what we do. It is when we design our lives around our purpose, and when **our passion takes over our pain**. In my experience, it is when my thoughts, emotions and actions are attuned to my passion. It is also that moment of jumping out of bed with excitement to be the solution to someone's problem. Or that moment of feeling satisfied with giving my best to change lives. This is what makes my life meaningful and purposeful. Going by Martin Seligman's definition of meaning, it gives me the confidence to know that I "**belong to, or am serving** something that I believe is bigger than the self." It is what makes me thrive!

> **Those who know their purpose and yet are
> distracted from it may end life feeling regrets
> and being angry with themselves.**

Testing the authenticity of passion and purpose

- What is the reason why you do what you do?
- Why do you go to work? For money, passion or both?
- If you were to be asked to deliver your services for free, would you still do it?
- Do you really enjoy what you do?
- Do you feel like without you, someone's life may be at risk?
- If you were to be awakened in the middle of the night to go to your job, would you happily go?

These are some of the questions I asked myself when I was battling with the question of whether I was genuinely happy with what I was doing. I wanted to know if it was my life's purpose and whether I was passionate enough about my job.

Before now, I was a community support worker, a job I had been doing for over eight years. I ditched my willingness to pursue a career in management after I completed my master's degree. From the moment I started providing care and support in a care home for the elderly, many people thought I had gone crazy. They mocked me for settling for a job they labelled a 'low-skilled and dirty job'. But who really cared? I loved my job! Supporting the elderly was a passion which I developed living with my granny and caring for her. When she passed away, I felt obligated to continue giving back my services to the elderly, as a payback for the relentless sacrifices my granny gave to me. Providing care and support was much more than the eyes could see. It was meaningful to me, and each time I saw the difference I was making in people's lives, I felt satisfied. Although it wasn't a well-paid job, with inflexible shift times, I would gladly do the job any day, anytime and even for free!

I also held varied positions as carer/support worker, senior support worker, supervisor and even a cleaner. Yes! I didn't even mind cleaning, so long as I was enjoying it. Just like writing, cleaning is therapeutic to me because it soothes me whenever I am stressed. So, if you need some help with cleaning, I am up for it!! The point I am driving at is that you can still be happy with your job, irrespective of what it is. What gives you the inner satisfaction that money can't buy?

> **Would you step forward and achieve your
> dreams or would you take them with you
> to the grave?**

Our Purpose Heals Our Pain

You would be surprised how your purpose can become your most valued therapy. The journey to uncover my purpose served as my most excellent therapeutic adventure in which I found immeasurable healing - a combination of my spiritual interactions with my physical life. Sometimes, I focused on building my spiritual life and interacted with nature and my religious beliefs. At other times, I applied the strengths acquired during my spiritual interactions to my day-to-day living, and this paid off. This healed my emotional wounds. The fact that I was no longer serving only myself, but also became the lifeboat of my kids, families and my *pain pals*, gave me the reason to be resilient. If I wasn't living for me, it was for the sake of these loved ones. Each day, I went to bed and woke up with a renewed mind and positive messages to motivate other *Pain Candidates*. My mind was full of positive ideas, such that there wasn't any space for those "ugly voices".

Today, I run training workshops and that became my mission – to create a supportive, inspiring and empowering environment to unlock personal growth and happiness. Writing this book is just in line with my mission – to help you to THRIVE by applying my 14 steps to turn your pain into gain. It is to help you develop a loving relationship with yourself and discover the hidden treasure that is within you; to enable you to live the life that you want. I love doing what I do, and the fulfilling results it produces for me and others. Whatever your passion may be, if you focus on it, it will heal your pain.

Our passion becomes our purpose, and our purpose becomes an anchor to a lasting recovery.

You Can Get Back on Track

Do you feel you are off track and can't seem to accomplish anything? We *Pain Candidates* usually feel like we don't have what it takes to become what we want. But that is not true. You don't need money, qualifications or professional connections to live your purpose. All you need is the willingness and determination to become what you want to become. With these two assets, all the others will follow. Maybe you were already living a purposeful life until that pain knocked you off track. The good news is that you can still get back on track if you choose to. If you had always wanted to become a medical doctor because you wanted to save lives, nothing is stopping you except you. The journey might be longer, but with willingness and determination, you will get there! Do you want to create your own business or gain employment in a company with services that align with your passion? You would be surprised that while you spend years talking about that dream or purpose, others are achieving theirs. So, stop talking about it; just do it! As Bev James puts it, **"You either do it or ditch it!"**

**It is crucial to find a job in something
enjoyable to you, which pays your bills,
satisfies your spirit, and makes others happy.**

Turning Disability into Gain of Ability

If there is one person whose life's story dragged me out of my comfort zone, that person is Nicholas James Vujicic. Nicholas is an Australian preacher and renowned motivational speaker, born without arms and legs. He is just one of the many who have chosen the path of turning their Pain of disability into Gain of ability for others.

Reading Nicholas's inspiring book, *Life without Limits*, I found he didn't just overcome his disability to live independently but also became emotionally, financially, spiritually and socially wealthy. He is living a thriving life and travelling the world, transforming the lives of others. The story of his physical disability and the emotional battles that rocked his life made me believe that life is indeed 10% what happens to us and 90% what we make of it. He mentioned that,

"For the longest, loneliest time, I wondered if there was anyone on earth like me, and whether there was any purpose to my life other than pain and humiliation."

And Nicholas successfully turned his pain and humiliation to gain. His key message is that the most valuable goal for anyone is to find and live their purpose on earth despite the challenges or ostensibly impossible odds that may stand in the way. As *Pain Candidates*, we often focus on our disability instead of our abilities. So, what limitations are you placing on your strengths? Have you learned from your experiences? What can you do with your talents? Don't be surprised that someone, right now, is counting on you as a source of inspiration to keep living. Let your purpose in life be their foundation of hope. When we create solutions to problems, we do not only change people's lives, we also make our lives meaningful and leave a positive legacy for future generations.

The most valuable goal for anyone is to find and
live their purpose on earth despite the challenges
or ostensibly impossible odds that may stand in
the way.

It's Never too Late

My son keeps yoyoing around what he wants to choose as a
career. One minute he wants to be a medical doctor because
he enjoys science and loves helping people, the next minute,
he wants to do business because he likes the flexibility and
human interaction too, then in another minute, he wants to
be an engineer because he loves creating stuff. I have been
encouraging him to choose without any coercion. It should
be something he loves, and which can change lives. I am
avoiding the temptation of telling him what to do because it
is about him, not me. It can be very frustrating if he picks a
career just because he wants to please anyone, gets to the top
and finds out that it wasn't for him. That may require him
to start all over again, and this can be painful! You might be
thinking, "This is my dilemma". And I must agree that it can
be challenging to make such a dramatic shift. Nevertheless,
like I always tell my *pain pals*, it is better to start all over again
and achieve your dream than to take the dream with you to
the grave. Therefore, it's never too late to pursue your dream
in life. Now that you know the importance of your purpose
in life, what would you say is your purpose? Are you already
living it? If not, can you think of how to accomplish it?

Unfortunately, one of the barriers that prevent us from
finding and living our purpose in life is our thought pattern,

which we shall talk about in our next chapter. Our limiting beliefs are like aggressive weeds that overtake our lives, choking any seed (ideas) that we attempt to sow, and killing our dreams. As *Pain Candidates,* sometimes our problem is not because we don't know what we want or how to have it; rather, it's because our distorted thinking pattern is controlling us. It's like the voice of a nagging and sceptical mother, continually telling a child that, "You can't do this – you can't do that". These damning voices can become like bees in your mind, buzzing around and irritating everything in your life. But there comes a time when you need to silence the noise by using every means possible.

Remember, all you need is the willingness and determination, and you're good to go!

CHAPTER 6

Step 4: Thinking Pattern

"The world as we have created it is a process of our thinking. It cannot be changed without changing our thinking."
Albert Einstein

Nothing can be more annoying than thinking that you own your house and life, only to find out that someone else does. You find yourself at loggerheads with this nasty visitor, and try to maintain control, but sadly, you're constantly conquered. That is how powerful our thought pattern can be.

Our thinking pattern is just our manner of thinking which may take us to the right or wrong path in life. Every time I attempted to make an audacious move and direct my path, my limiting thoughts and emotions overpowered me, sapping every ounce of energy, and leaving me depleted like an airless balloon. "Peggy, how long are you going to fight this?" I questioned myself. And with a resolute response, I said, "As long as I live and until I win!" I was determined not to join those who had let their irrational thoughts kill their dreams, but to feature amongst those who diligently guarded their minds and made the world a better place.

Look around you – What can you see? For me, I can see my clothes, mobile phone, a laptop, a TV, my sofa, books, video games, and many others. Everything you see around you is a product of someone's thought or idea. The world as we see it has become a global village, thanks to the science and technology which have revolutionised our lifestyle. What would life have been during this Covid-19 without technology? With social media, you can have visual communication with a loved one thousands of miles away. With the aid of cars and aircraft, you can be in another country within minutes or hours. With online shopping, you can order an item and get it delivered immediately. With medical science, illnesses are easily diagnosed and treated. All these fantastic products and services are created from people's ideas or our thoughts. We are always thinking; even when we're asleep, our thoughts play back to us. In my view, thinking is like oxygen, and we can't survive without it. Right now, you may be thinking of enrolling in a college course, starting a new job, having a new relationship, leaving an abusive relationship, stopping that addiction, saving more money, and the list goes on. So, what we think about every day controls our lives and our world. But surprisingly, it is the least valued element of our lives. As *Pain Candidates*, we don't get the chance to evaluate the importance and impact of our thought pattern on every area of our lives.

In our quest to turn our pain into gain, we cannot ignore our thought pattern because the quality of our thoughts determines the quality of our lives. The greatest asset of life is a healthy mind and before we thrive, we must be able to THINK. This means, being able to process information rationally, controlling our thought pattern to be aligned with our values, goals, and happiness. When we fail to do this, we waste our time and energy thinking 'rubbish or nothing' which lead us to a 'rubbish or nothing life'. Life-changing or positive ideas cannot be planted and sustained on a constantly negative mind. As Blaise Pascal once said,

"You are today where the thoughts of yesterday have brought you and you will be tomorrow where the thoughts of today take you."

When we cultivate the habit of irrational thinking, we end up with negative results. From experience, it is always tempting to dwell on the past: our mistakes and failures, missed opportunities, wickedness and weaknesses of others, and blaming people and events for our lives. Going through my 'messed-up' life, I didn't know this principle: "Thought is equal to results", so I needed to educate myself. The success of transforming my mind was thanks to some great books. I read books like **Mind Power** by James Borg; **A new guide to rational living** by Albert Ellis; **The power of subconscious mind** by Joseph Murphy and others. These books helped me understood the extent to which my unhealthy and painful thought patterns were messing up my life. I needed to know the origin of this limiting mindset to appropriately deal with it.

It Comes from a Source

Where do we get our thought patterns from, or why do we think the way we do?

We were not born with negative or positive thought patterns. Neither is anyone born with low or high self-esteem. These are often learned from someone or something. Looking back at my childhood life and my painful past, people and events shaped my thought pattern. My granny, family members, the community, friends, my schoolteachers, and my painful encounters made me think, talk and act the way I did. Although my granny instilled positive values in me, like respect, love, sharing, caring, forgiveness, honesty, and the like, I still grew up feeling less valued because of my experiences. My community stigmatised me, kids avoided me, and my teachers paid no attention to me. Others asserted that I was abnormal and unfit to share the same class with other kids.

Surprisingly, I faced the same stigma within my family circles. I found that I was often discriminated against and treated with scorn each time I visited some of my relatives. While the kids could eat anything they wanted, sit anywhere in the house, and their needs were provided for, I was restricted to specific areas in the home and left to starve. I did all the difficult household chores and became an easy target to be falsely accused and flogged. These made me develop an inferiority mindset which affected my confidence, self-esteem and thought pattern. This subservience mentality continued through my teenage and adulthood. My submissiveness and desire for validation caused me to trust easily, forgive quickly, be easily intimidated, and I constantly took the blame, wanting to please others to my own detriment. The more I did that, the more I devalued myself and the more I was emotionally exhausted.

After my relationship breakup, my painful childhood and adulthood encounters couldn't stop ringing in my head.

The negative voices, limiting beliefs, flashbacks, name-calling, blackmailing and self-blaming were dominating my thoughts, and it was becoming tiring and debilitating. I am sure you might have had a similar experience which has affected you psychologically. It is likely that we might be stuck in the pain unless we choose to recondition our minds, to see that we can learn a whole lot of positives (gain) in our suffering. Also, we could unconsciously be surrendering our lives to the mercy of these negative experiences and thought patterns, which only bring us misery. Thus, it is vital to reset our mental programming and re-evaluate the results of our thoughts, otherwise, we stifle our growth.

People often ask me whether I hold a grudge against anyone who mistreated me, and my answer has always been, "Absolutely not!" In any case, all these people, consciously or unconsciously, added value to my life. Apart from the life skills learned, the experiences got me determined to excel academically and to always work hard to meet my needs. Another reason I bore no bitterness is that these people were also functioning within their limiting beliefs. Some of my relatives, for example, assumed that non-biological children were not regarded as part of the nuclear family, and ought to be treated differently. But as we know, such discrimination may leave children with lasting adverse effects. I always say, *every child deserves to be treated as a child. The child you love could grow up to never love you. But the child you reject may be the one to love and save you.* Why would a rejected child be so kind and loving? It is because that child understands the hidden treasure of rejection or pain. Therefore, it is psychologically rewarding to step away from the pain and focus on the gain.

> Irrespective of the source of your pain,
> developing an attitude of gratitude can
> heal you faster.

We May Believe It's True

You would be amazed how many people validate the veracity of limiting beliefs. We all suffer from entrenched belief systems which have inflicted untold pain with similar consequences. Surprisingly, we have had core beliefs about ourselves, people and events, and even when challenged, we refuse to blink. Our lives get centred around those core beliefs, and any attempt to recondition our minds may feel like doing the unthinkable. For instance, someone who believes that all men are abusers may never accept any valid contrary arguments. The fact that we have been believing something for decades, doesn't necessarily make it true. As mentioned in Chapter Four, once we become adults, we have the choice to take responsibility for our lives and that also means changing our generational irrational thought patterns. By doing so, we alter our lives from pain to gain.

During my recovery journey, I realised that holding on to limiting beliefs and negative thoughts hampered my life's transformation. This challenged me to step out of my comfort zone and belief system to change my life. Thus, I shifted my thought pattern to restart my life. Writing this book is a way of helping any *Pain Candidate* to have a *mental rebirth* - A change that will enable them to take back control of their lives, unlock their passions and potential, turn that pain into gain and move from a surviving life to a thriving life. Remember:

> You are the captain of your thoughts, and
> you are too precious to allow unhealthy
> thoughts to ruin your life.

Are You OVERTHINKING?

Just as I was about to dispute the assertion by psychologists that a human being, on average, thinks around 60,000 – 80,000 thoughts per day, my phone went ding! It was a message that read, "I don't think she'll make it." And it ended with a crying face emoji. In less than five minutes, I had already had about 60 thoughts and counting. And the most intriguing finding is that the first thought was negative, and it spiralled into other negative ideas.

Around that time, my mum was admitted to hospital, and after reading that message, the first thought was, "**My mum is going to die**", and my inner chatter started as follows:

"...Does that mean she is going to die? The last time she was admitted we knew she wasn't going to make it, so perhaps her time is up. How would I travel? I don't think my job will grant me leave because I used all my annual leave. I don't even have the money... What about the kids? It will be too much work for their aunty to look after them. Pat may want to stay home alone, but I can't leave him, he's still a minor. I would really love to travel with them, but it's costly. Their school won't permit them to travel. Oh! I need to vaccinate them. My friend's daughter came back with chronic malaria. I don't want that to happen to the kids. What will my family be thinking about the funeral?

I bet Uncle George should be pleased because he always had a beef against Mum... I am ready for him if he dares want to hijack the funeral. I remember Mum's favourite songs to play on that day..."

I sat with my eyes staring at the wall, but a whole lot ravaging my mind. It's not as if I don't love my mum; I love her so dearly and she knows it. She also suffers from heart malfunction, and if there is one thing I do not joke about, it is her medical care. You may wonder why I was overshadowed by negative thoughts when I had not even investigated the reason behind such a text. You may also ask why I did not think rationally or why I could not dispute the initial thought. Well, it is because that is the way the human mind functions. This is more peculiar in situations where the person has become an irrational thinker. Unfortunately, as those negative thoughts were speeding in and out of my mind, my negative emotions were also mounting. I was feeling stressed, tearful, anxious, angry, frustrated and guilty, and, within minutes, was looking exhausted and pale.

After acting out what I called my *mental mini movie* and wiping away a few tears, I finally gathered the courage to get more details. I rang my mum's phone as always, hoping that this time my sister would answer. Surprisingly, I got a loud, "Hello!" as my mum screamed energetically. "Mum, is that you?" I asked. "Yes, it's me. I just finished a church meeting with my fellow ladies", she responded. "How are you feeling?" I asked. "I am fine! I was discharged yesterday, and I am recovering very well", she replied. Phew! "What was all that negative thinking about?" I asked myself as I sat at the same spot, recovering from my self-inflicted emotional pain. At that moment, I noticed that the text message was from an unregistered number. Upon dialling it, I realised it was an old acquaintance who was upset because her best friend couldn't make it to her wedding. The only reason the message mistakenly came to me was that her best friend's name also starts with a P, and it was next to my name on her phone. I couldn't stop beating myself up for such a self-inflicted trauma – all because of? - **My Painful Thinking Pattern.**

That is the same way our distorted thoughts about ourselves, people and events can leave us paralysed with negative emotions. Anything you connect with through your five senses generates a thought, which could be negative or positive. As we all know, each day brings its worries and disappointments. We worry about Covid-19, our kids, partners, family members, our jobs, health, finances, political events, natural disasters, and the like. Speaking with my *pain pals*, it appears everyone seems to have their own painful, harmful, or distorted thinking pattern. Aaron Becks (1976) and David Burns (1980) identified painful, harmful, or distorted patterns, some of which may resonate with ours. I have coined these patterns with a word – **OVERTHINKING** – as shown below.

O – Overgeneralisation
V – Valid Thinking
E – Either/or Thinking
R – Rigid Thinking
T – Typify Thinking
H – History Thinking

I – Individualised Thinking
N – Negative Thinking
K – Knowing-all Thinking
I – Illusionary Thinking
N – Negative Anticipation
G – Guilt

Before we delve into highlighting these thinking patterns, it is worth noting that any thought you conceive, and attention given to it, creates a healthy or an unhealthy mind and body. This is because each thought generates a corresponding emotional response, which also creates brain chemicals that are released into the bloodstream. I love the way James Borg puts it in various parts in his book - *Mind Power*. He says,

> **"Our brain is like a 'pharmacy' which is
> open 24/7, and by how we choose to think,
> we instruct it to dispense either good or
> bad chemicals…"**

When we think rationally and positively, we generate positive emotions like joy, gratitude, forgiveness, trust, optimism, confidence, enthusiasm, love, inspiration, etc. These emotions produce 'feel good' chemicals in the brain like endorphins, oxytocin, serotonin, and dopamine. These 'feel good' chemicals also play varied functions like releasing energy, motivation, bonding; it relieves body pain, stress, anxiety, and depression and regulates our blood pressure and the like. A visual image can be something like this, with a smiling face or healthy and happy mind and body.

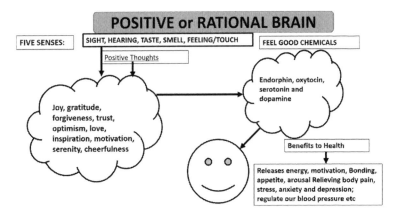

On the other hand, when we continuously think irrationally and negatively, we generate negative emotions like sadness, doubt, hatred, guilt, frustration, fear, jealousy, revenge, grief, pessimism, and others. These produce 'feel bad' chemicals in the brain like cortisol and adrenaline, also known as the stress hormones. These stress hormones increase heart rate and blood pressure, increase sugar in the bloodstream, boost energy, etc. It is worth mentioning that hormones like adrenaline prepare us to fight or flight a danger. Cortisol also regulates blood sugar, metabolism, salt, and water balance, and helps foetal development. However, when both hormones are released continuously into the bloodstream, it puts the body at higher risk of developing health issues. Some of these could be anxiety, depression, headaches, heart disease, sleep problems, weight gain and the like.[5] So we may end up with a sad face or unhealthy mind and body.

---

[5] www.mayoclinic.org

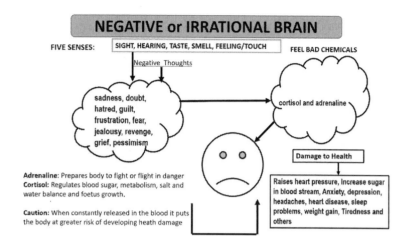

Therefore, we need to endeavour not to overthink. It is also worthy to note that having some of these distorted thinking patterns to the extreme could be a sign of mental illness, which needs medical attention. We should never be shy to seek help and live the life that we were born to live. No one was born to OVERTHINK and ruin their lives.

O - Overgeneralisation

Overgeneralisation is a cognitive distortion where we may use one experience to generalise all experiences (present and future). As *Pain Candidates*, just because we messed up once, or something happened once, or we did something wrong a few times does not mean it happens **always** or will happen **always**. Also, the fact that someone treated us badly doesn't mean **everybody** will mistreat us. Unfortunately, we are fond of overgeneralising, using words like *always*, *everyone, nobody, all the time, never, you people,* etc. We make statements like:

- **No one** feels my pain or understands me or believes me!
- **Nobody** ever listens to what I say.
- **All men** are abusers and pathetic liars!
- I **always** mess up in job interviews.
- I **never** get anything right.
- The **world** is an evil place.

What do you think about this pattern? It puts everyone in a single box and creates the impression that nobody cares! It also stops you from speaking up and seeking help. Likewise, it takes away your confidence and the opportunity to take risks, unlock your passion and potential, and thrive. It also offers no optimism and, most especially, it generates negative emotions. Reread the list and notice your emotional reaction.

In our Pain to Gain journey, we need to treat people, behaviours, and events separately. Just like there are bad people out there, there are also good and great people. Just like you have some weaknesses, you also have some strengths. The fact that you made a mistake a few times does not mean you will make mistakes all the time. And even if you make mistakes 'always', that is not the end of the world. Remember, in every mistake you make, there's a lesson you learn, and it is empowering to focus on the lesson. In addition, the fact that someone or a few people did not believe what you said, doesn't mean you are wrong or there is no one to listen to you. Someone may not agree with your opinion or belief, but it does not negate the fact that your idea is valued. Similarly, the fact that a relationship(s) did not work out doesn't mean everyone is abusive and a liar. One person might be a Pain, while another is a Gain. Thus, it is crucial to identify this thinking pattern, challenge it and replace it with positive or constructive ones.

V - Valid Thinking

I chose to call it this way because my *pain pals* and you, the reader, would understand better. On many occasions, I hear statements like, "What I feel is valid, or what I feel is true." Psychologists refer to this as emotional reasoning. It is the thinking pattern that makes us believe that whatever we feel is real, accurate or valid. We typically think that the emotions we generate are proof of reality. For example, the fact that I may not feel excited about going out for a romantic date is not proof that the date will not be successful. Also, the fact that you are feeling anxious about a job interview is not evidence that you won't get the job. Similarly, the fact that you feel lonely does not mean no one cares about you or loves you. Or the fact that you feel overwhelmed by something doesn't mean you can't handle it. Just like our gut feeling or wisdom, our emotional state must be questioned and objectively analysed before we draw any conclusion.

Remember, we mentioned that every feeling begins with a thought. And from sharing my experiences about my mum, we know that our thoughts are not always accurate – they are just thoughts! Someone with a valid thinking pattern can get withdrawn, procrastinate, become fearful, shy, pessimistic, paranoid about people and events and refuse to take risks.

They may start looking for evidence to justify the thought by misinterpreting messages or 'connecting dots' to suit their beliefs. You may make statements like, "I knew I wasn't going to get the job, that's why I missed my bus to attend the interview." Meanwhile, nervousness could have caused you to drag your feet and thus, you missed the bus and the job opportunity. So, if we aim to thrive in every aspect of our lives, we should also need to learn to challenge our emotional reasoning. For some, it can only be achieved by seeking professional help. For others, we can be able to think, feel and behave rationally just by asking simple questions like, "How true is this feeling?" or "What are the facts to justify this feeling?" The more you challenge your feelings, the less negative impact it has on your wellbeing (Physical, psychological, financial, spiritual, intellectual etc.).

E - Either/or Thinking

Psychologists would refer to this as polarized thinking or splitting. With this cognitive distortion pattern, we view behaviours, expectations, and events at extremes: something is either black or white; right or wrong; good or bad; all or nothing. There are no grey areas. As *Pain Candidates*, we may make statements like:

- My life is a complete mess.
- My partner is utterly useless.
- My friend is perfect.
- If I don't get that job, I won't be bothered to look for another one.
- It is either she calls me, or I block her number.

- It is either I am promoted to that managerial position, or I am out.
- It is either she apologises or she can stop talking to me.
- I either pass that driving test this time, or I give up.
- We are in for something, or we are out.

What is your view on this thought pattern? In my opinion, it is a pattern that has a mixture of emotions – frustration, anger, guilt, revenge, pessimism, love, trust, confidence, optimism, determination, etc. Interestingly, a feeling can immediately switch to an extreme. In a relationship, for example, love can instantly turn into hatred, if there wasn't any room for flaws. Life, as we know, is not perfect. You and I are not perfect; neither are our friends and families. Also, events and expectations in life may never be exactly as we want them. We will have bad days, good days, and so-so days. Therefore, we should not just give up because we didn't get it right. Turning our Pain into Gain requires us to be human, and never to give up until we're satisfied with ourselves. Like Vince Lombardi puts it, "**Winners never quit, and quitters never win.**" Thus, to maintain the momentum, it is essential to create leeway for people's behaviours, events, and results in our lives. Also, it is vital to appreciate and celebrate our micro wins, strengths and abilities, and the kind gestures of others. Be willing to tell yourself that, "Although I wasn't successful in getting that job, I believe I've got the skills and I will search for other opportunities." That is optimism! And this thinking pattern will eventually lead you to turn your Pain of disappointment to Gain of accomplishment.

R - Rigid Thinking

This distorted thinking pattern is also known as the *should or must* thinking pattern. Based on our respective beliefs and values, we usually assume that people, behaviours, results, events, and the world **should, must, ought to, and have to** be a specific way. In the event of this not happening, we quickly become angry, frustrated and even guilty. Like either/ or thinking, there is no flexibility of thoughts – it is a MUST!

I am sure you are familiar with statements like:

- My kids **must** perform well.
- My partner **should** behave in such and such a way.
- My boss **must** treat me well.
- I **must** lose weight.
- I **should not** have gotten into that relationship.
- I **should** be likeable.
- I **should** have been in such and such a position by now.
- She **should** be married by now.
- **If only** I had the money, qualification, or experience.
- **If only** I had listened to my friends.

These statements are more rigid and regrettable, and they do nothing other than add to our pain. As *Pain Candidates*, we may sometimes make these rigid statements believing they motivate; rather, most serve as demotivation. For example, "I **must** lose weight." That means it is an absolute – no ifs, no buts. However, it could also put us under pressure to prove a point, which, if not achieved, might leave us feeling guilty, angry and frustrated. In addition, it can kill our self-esteem and confidence and stifle our growth, especially if we believe we lack the ability to succeed. Besides, these inflexible statements may affect our relationships with others, especially if they don't meet our expectations and standards. Remember, in life, things will not always go as planned because we have no control over people's behaviours, events, and results.

Another thing to mention is that rigid statements leave us vulnerable because we feel like we deserved to be punished for not accomplishing a goal. So, to preserve our mental sanity, it is essential to avoid guilt, frustration, and anger by watching the words we use in our communications. Also, we need to be more tolerant in the ways in which we communicate about ourselves to feel empowered and be in control. Some examples of tolerant and empowering self-communications include:

- I **would** love my kids to perform well so I may need to put some support in place.
- It **would** be great if my boss promotes me, so I need to keep doing my best.
- **Although** I wouldn't have gotten into that relationship, I am glad I learned some lessons. I am using these lessons to move on.
- I **understand** it is great to be kind to people, so I am working towards that.

When you avoid rigidity and regrets in your statements, you create hope and the willingness to re-strategize and achieve the required results. I call these "action-oriented statements" based on my experiences as these helped me to develop plans that turned my painful thinking into gainful thinking.

T- Typify Thinking

Who can escape this thinking pattern? Psychologists refer to it as labelling. I was prompted to call it Typify thinking because of what I experienced in one of my recovery training sessions. As mentioned in Chapter Two, *Pain Candidates* usually find it easier to list their weaknesses than strengths. This holds true, to a large extent, to everyone regardless of our circumstances. If I ask you now to tell me ten good things about you, you may have to scratch your head a little, with a few Um…, Err and Uh… But don't worry, you're not alone because easily identifying our strengths and abilities comes with practice. In this recovery training, we were attempting to list some of our irrational beliefs so that we could challenge ourselves to replace them with rational ones. Then, the trainer called out some negative labels or statements like:

- I am a **failure**
- I am a **bad** cook
- I am **useless**
- I am **stupid**
- He's an **asshole**
- She's **hopeless**
- I am a **bad parent**
- I am **rubbish** at my job
- I am **ugly**
- She's a **bitch**
- He's a little **devil**
- I am **foolish**

Please don't read it twice, its Traumatising!

I wasn't much interested in the above labels because they sounded quite distressing. But what caught my attention were the responses my *Pain Pals* were throwing back. I heard statements like:

- That's exactly me!
- That describes me.
- That's typical of me.
- That typifies me.
- That characterises me
- That's exactly what my partner is.

Therefore, based on our irrational views, we typify or characterise ourselves and others with false labels. Sadly, we live in a highly judgmental world, where people would do everything possible to make us feel inadequate. And some of these labels would start early on in our childhood, through to teenage and adulthood. Because we have heard these negative tags repeatedly, we then begin to believe them and act the same. At times, the negative tags lead us to decline compliments or even question our performance. Before I found my true self, it was typical for me to doubt or deny compliments. For instance, each time someone told me "you're beautiful", I would respond by questioning; "are you sure?" This is a typical example of constant negative tagging which leads someone to normalise the tags and doubt their true self. A proper response to such a compliment could be "thank you!"

The effects of normalising negative labels are that we generate associated feelings such as low self-esteem, disappointment, pessimism, anger, resentment, anxiety and being less motivated to try new things, which justify the labels. Remember that people's perception of you is not your reality. I may come across as stupid, but I am not stupid. In the same way, you could have failed in something, yet that doesn't make you a failure. Or more still, you might not know how to cook a specific meal, but that does not make you a bad cook. A more positive approach is to tell yourself that, "I would love to cook a meal, so I am determined to learn the recipe." Or "Although I didn't accomplish that specific goal, I learned some lessons and I'm using it to perform better next time." When you think this way, it encourages you and others to value and believe in yourselves. It helps you to turn painful tags to gainful tags.

H- History Thinking

As *Pain Candidates,* this is another distorted thinking pattern that we might all be guilty of. Psychologists refer to it as Blaming. I call it history thinking because blaming is often based on past behaviours or events with a negative outcome. In my view, anything that has already happened is considered history; in the past. It may not be forgotten, but nothing changes the fact that it has occurred, and the damage has already been done. We could only repair the damage but would never reverse the original position. So, rather than focus on the loss and blaming yourself or others for the havoc, it is much healthier to focus on the way forward – solution.

In Chapter Four, we talked at length on the pain of the blame game and the gain of accepting responsibility for our lives. There is no point lamenting or clinging to the past and not letting it go. We may feel more depressed by continuously using statements like: "if only I had", "I could have", "I should have", "I wish I" "It's her fault", "It's my fault". Again, these are statements of regret which only leave us angry and resentful. It is true that the results we got from the past experiences were not pleasant, but what are you doing with the lessons learned? What are you doing with your strength toolbox? Should you be using it to move forward or stay at the same spot bemoaning? The past has come and gone. What are you doing now to change your future? Think about it.

I - Individualised Thinking

This thinking pattern is psychologically referred to as personalising or personalisation. This is when we believe that everything others do or say is as a result of our actions or omissions. Consequently, we appropriate their behaviour, with the tendency of shouldering responsibility for people's actions or negative results. For example, you ask a friend to accompany you to a birthday party, and when your friend returned home, her partner, out of jealousy, physically assaulted her. So, you take the blame that if you hadn't invited her, that wouldn't have happened. Common! It is not your fault that your friend's partner chose to be abusive.

I must confess that I used to struggle with this thinking pattern before my *mental rebirth*. If I sent someone a message, for example, and they didn't reply immediately, my individualised thinking would begin. I would ask myself,

"Why haven't I gotten a reply? Did I do or say something wrong? Maybe my content was meaningless..." And I would usually begin to apologise for nothing. I might send another message saying, "Please, if I said something wrong, forgive me. I was only suggesting." Gosh! What a Painful Thinking! And what about speaking to someone you know, and not receiving a response? I am sure you are familiar with that. This happens a lot in relationships, especially when you greet your partner and all he/she does is to blank at you. The immediate thought would be – did I do something wrong? Or you may begin to assume justifications for their behaviours.

As *Pain Candidates,* we don't have to take blame unnecessarily. Once we have said or done what is right, there is no point worrying about it. It is the receiver's choice to interpret our message, action, or omission the way they want. However, their interpretation shouldn't change our reality. It is important to note that the recipient of our communications or actions might just be going through tough times which require them to take some personal breathing space. Thus, a wrong conclusion might leave us more vulnerable and at the begging end.

N – Negative Thinking

The name says it all – we are usually negative or pessimistic about people and events. Psychologists refer to this as mental filtering or magnification. This is when we take out negative details about someone or something and exaggerate it, filtering out all positive aspects of the person or thing. When this happens, we could end up with a distorted image, far from reality, and ignore anything positive.

When pain candidates assume negative thinking, we would usually need to be convinced that what we are thinking about is not realistic and might not materialise. Most often, we utter conclusions that benefit our worldview. For instance, we may, by virtue of negative thinking, say the following: "I will never make it; I know I will never be selected for the job interview; I know I will never get the job; I am certain that person is evil; I will fail that exam; I won't find a partner" and so forth. This kind of thinking can further create a barrage of negative emotions like fear, anger, frustration, revenge, jealousy, guilt, low self-esteem, sleeplessness, and even suicidal thoughts. And sometimes, even after presenting valid justifications, we may still be stuck in our negative cycle. As aforementioned, these feelings may cause physical health challenges like high blood pressure, heart disease, stroke and others which might limit our potential to live a desired life. Our journey from pain to gain requires us to be unbiased, and to have realistic expectations about people, events and results in our lives. Lack of this could limit your personal and career development.

K - Know- It- All Thinking

"Do you know people who always jump to conclusions claiming they know how you think or feel?" This pattern describes such people and psychologists refer to this pattern as jumping to conclusion or mind-reading. Besides, people who exhibit such distortions do not always bother to find out if their assertions are justified or truthful. When pain candidates assume such distortions, they find it difficult to acknowledge their weaknesses, show remorse or take ownership of their actions and omissions but insist on being always right.

During training sessions with pain candidates, I noticed such attitudes expressed in the following examples: My partner is the know-it-all boss. My partner thinks he can tell me exactly what I want, but he's always wrong! My partner always completes my sentences, and I hate it. My sister believes I despise her, but that's not true. I have concluded that she doesn't love me. I can't seem to meet my partner's goalposts because he thinks I am always wrong. I don't want another relationship because it's not going to last. My boss doesn't like me; he thinks I am rubbish.

Interestingly, we usually conclude without bothering to find out if our assertion is true or not. If I assume and make you a cup of tea, when in fact, you need a cup of coffee, have I met your need? Absolutely not! You may sympathise and drink the tea, but deep within, you're not satisfied. That is similar to what happens in relationships where needs are not met, or emotional bruises are created because of jumping to conclusion. There is no harm in listening to people's concerns and asking questions before attempting to provide solutions.

With this thought pattern, we may hardly acknowledge our weaknesses or show remorse for our actions or omissions. And thus, we are right! In response to our making tea instead of coffee, we might not say sorry but reaffirm our "rightness", for instance, by saying "well, you always drink tea, so what's wrong with that?" Really? I may always drink tea, but I want to drink coffee today! I am human, and my needs do change! This thinking pattern inhibits healthy relationships, communication and understanding. This is because if you have friends or family members who feel as if you rarely allow them to express themselves or draw false conclusions, they might start to distance themselves from you. And what is life without healthy relationships?

I - Illusionary Thinking

Imagine that it's Monday morning and whilst you are preparing for a job interview, I knock on your door and inform you that you won't get the job because you're going to have an accident and not make it to the interview. If you believe me, would you still attend the interview? Well, you may, but many would not. Why? Because they believe in fortune-telling and have the illusion that whatever is said, is true. This thought pattern is called fortune-telling, and it is like mind-reading/jumping to conclusion and emotional reasoning. Based on our beliefs and values, we turn predictions or assumptions into facts. I do understand that there are professional fortune-tellers. However, we need to be aware that we could end up creating self-fulfilling prophecies by virtue of our compliance. For example, in the scenario above, if you obeyed what I said and didn't attend the interview, would you get the job? The answer is no! Would you have turned the illusion into reality? An emphatic yes! Because after all, you haven't gotten the job! Therefore, as *Pain Candidates*, we may hold back from opportunities because of the belief that someone or something is not going to favour us. We fail to recondition our minds, seek professional help, read books, enrol at college, start a relationship or business and make an investment because we believe that we're destined to fail. But how can you know if you've not tried? Even if you tried once or twice and didn't succeed, can you try again? Perhaps that distorted thinking is blocking your success.

It is also important to note that this thought pattern exerts huge emotional damage on its adherent. In our case as pain candidates, the emotional damage will include living in constant fear, doubt, frustration, shame, anger, procrastination, low self-esteem, etc. Besides, our physical, emotional, spiritual, financial, intellectual and career growths may be hindered. Remember, you were not born to live a mediocre life. You have what it takes to become who you want to be. So, Go For It!

N- Negative Anticipation

This is referred to by psychologists as Catastrophising. This thought pattern would leave us imagining the worst whenever something occurs. This is the thought pattern that left me traumatised after reading the message, "I don't think she'll be able to make it". In my mind, I pictured the worst – the dead body, the casket, wailing, funeral procession and the like. We do have daily events which may create negative anticipation, for example, you're told there is a ghastly accident in your child's school - what first comes to your mind? You can't find your purse or phone – what's the thought? You can't reach your teenage child after a night's party – what comes to your mind? You suddenly discover a lump on your body – what's the thought? Your partner doesn't return home as expected – what comes to your mind?

Hey! We are human! And it is natural to panic when we are faced with the unexpected. However, we must be able to control our minds by arresting any negative thought from spiralling into more negative thoughts. As mentioned, we need to question the validity of our views and get the facts right before we conclude. Catastrophising also involves asking the "what if" question. What if I fail? What if he doesn't like me? What if I have an accident? These "what if" questions, in my opinion, are good because they serve as prompts to set up contingency plans. It is like realistic pessimism, which is quite common in business or governmental organisations. As part of a business's continuity strategy, an action plan would always be in place for the unexpected to ensure that the company is prepared to manage any unexpected outcomes. Taking out insurance is another way of dealing with the "what ifs" aspect of this thought pattern. Although the occurrence of the unexpected is unlikely, the "what ifs" provide a safety net which leads to stability and peace of mind. Thus, rational "what if" is gainful!

Nevertheless, "What ifs" become problematic when applied irrationally. The irrational "what if" may lead us to be stuck in our negatives and afraid of growth. For example, refusing to drive your car because you're scared of having an accident or refusing to seek employment because you are too scared to make mistakes. When these occur, you may limit your growth and happiness. Interestingly, every success in life involves risk-taking and every opportunity comes with a price. An appropriate approach is to acknowledge the risk, assess it and put preventive measures in place, while also enjoying the great benefits that accompany it. Therefore, if you cultivate the habit of seeing the Gain in every Pain, you'll turn any Pain into Gain.

G - Guilt

The feeling of guilt may be distorted thinking, as well as negative emotions generated by all the above patterns. Guilt accompanies blame or criticism. Guilt makes us blame or criticise ourselves or others for mishaps. As mentioned earlier, we all make mistakes and sometimes, we wilfully execute actions that may be detrimental to ourselves and others due to our irrational thought patterns and negative emotions. When these happen, we may develop a strong sense of guilt, which, if not resolved, may ignite other emotions like sadness, worthlessness and even feeling suicidal. Moreover, our environment (people) can use our good-faith or bad-faith actions to build guilt in us which opens a plethora of negativity with damaging psychological effects, which can be a deterrent towards our personal growth. Have you ever done something which you thought was helping someone, but they turned it against you? How did you feel? Awful, I should think; and for me, that's the worst feeling ever. As pain candidates, we are often accused falsely which may leave us feeling helpless, self-blaming and emotionally drained. However, we should find comfort in our truth, because we know that we acted in good faith. And like the saying – Truth always prevails.

One lesson I have learned in my recovery journey is to always practice behaviour-critiquing. I find it more empowering to critique my behaviour than criticising myself (Peggy). This means, rather than beating and negatively labelling myself over unproductive behaviour, I focused more on identifying what is not right and suggesting alternative ways of acting better.

That is why when I miss an appointment, instead of cursing and tagging myself, I look in the mirror and say, *"Peggy, I love you, but I dislike your poor time-management skill. You need to work on it, else you will miss opportunities. Next time, ensure to turn up 10 minutes early."* The fact that I am willing to change is empowering because I believe that every mistake made is a learning curve and I'm using the lessons to become a better person. So instead of feeling guilty, I feel forgiven, hopeful, loving, enthusiastic and confident in myself. As a parent, I do also practice this with my kids whenever they misbehave. It is encouraging to tell a child that, *"I love you, but I don't like such and such behaviour. I am ready to help you deal with it because I would love to see you succeed in life."* Isn't that motivating? Likewise, I practice it with my friends, family members and I also encourage you to do the same.

So, my dear *Pain Candidates,* remember that in this journey called LIFE, people, events, and results will not always be pleasing. Remember, people will walk into our lives, make a mess and leave. On many occasions, we will blunder. You and I have done it before, and it may happen again. Is that a big deal? I would say, No! It is part of life. Even when our environment constantly makes us look stupid, we need to learn to accept the good and throw away the rest. As Winston Churchill rightly puts it;

> **"Success is not final; failure is not fatal: it is the courage to continue that counts."**

When we fall, we can rise, dust ourselves off and keep moving. Therefore, I ask you again, are you OVERTHINKING?

Our Pain to Gain journey requires us to challenge these distorted thought patterns, and if doing so requires medical attention, please do not hesitate. You would be glad to know that psychotherapy is not only recommended for people with severe mental illnesses. For all you know, mental illnesses are widespread, and psychological research shows that everyone will develop at least one diagnosable psychological disorder at some point in their life. According to the Diagnostic and Statistical Manual of Mental Disorders, there are nearly 300 mental disorders. And mental illness, just like other illnesses, doesn't discriminate; it can affect anyone, irrespective of race, gender or social status. While some mental illnesses are mild and have limited interference with our daily lives, others may be severe and debilitating. I am sure, going through the thinking patterns, you can identify with at least one of them. Although the impact of a specific distorted pattern could be minimal, if not addressed, it can deteriorate. For example, mental filtering can create a host of negative emotions like fear, anger, frustration, revenge, jealousy, guilt, low self-esteem, and sleeplessness. If not managed effectively, it may deteriorate into clinical depression and suicidal thoughts, which may be debilitating. Sadly enough, because mental illness is a stigmatized disease, many people feel ashamed to admit struggling with a mental health problem. Others, especially in black and Asian communities, don't even believe it exists. Mental health problems are nothing to be ashamed of, and prevention is always better than cure. That means our journey from Pain to Gain begins from the mind. You can turn that Painful thinking into Gainful thinking, thereby taking control of your life and your happiness. You can thrive again!

As a *Pain Candidate*, being fully aware of the damages that my distorted thinking has caused in my life, I cannot be grateful enough for my mental rebirth. I have indeed learned to be the boss of my thoughts and not the other way around. We need to learn to practice mind control – whether by taking a deep breath, counting backwards, walking away from a tense environment, challenging our thoughts, etc. - these are life-changing techniques to practice in our everyday life; learning to challenge our old ways of thinking. The next time you feel like your thought is taking you along the wrong track, just shout **"Mind control!"** It is a continuous journey and, with practice, practice and more practice, we can get even better. When you do, you will enjoy the peace and happiness that you so deserve in your life.

As we'll be sharing in the next chapter, forming a healthy thinking pattern accompanies healthy habits. Just like our phones, if we don't charge them, they run out of power and can be rendered unusable. Likewise, if we don't protect our phones, they can easily be damaged. Our habits would either charge or drain the battery of our minds, rendering it usable or useless.

If we know that we have control of our minds, or that we are responsible for our thinking patterns, we can easily choose the direction of our thoughts.

CHAPTER 7

Step 5: Healthy Habits

*A Healthy Habit is like a wheel that gets your
life rolling to your desired destination.*

Ponder for a moment! Did any physical or mental activities constitute part of your habit from the time you woke up from bed until now? What about the way you think, feel, talk, behave; or the way you brush your teeth, wash, dress, clean, cook, etc.? Are these activities done in similar or different ways? These questions have obvious responses because we are a species of habits which makes our daily life a combination of our feelings and behaviours. Also, everyone possesses unique habits which, as discussed earlier, have corresponding outcomes. The present result in our lives – happy or unhappy, fulfilled, or unfulfilled, negative, or positive – is the sum of our habits.

According to MacMillan Dictionary, a habit is *"something that you do often or regularly, often without thinking about it."* One of my habits is to sweep and tidy my living room, dining room and kitchen every night before going to bed. My kids cannot understand why I do what they now call, "Mum's cleaning ritual". Well, it is because it's a habit! Institutions would also have a way of functioning which is guided by rules or regulations, culture, style, and so on. The only difference is whether these habits are painful or gainful, healthy or unhealthy, productive or unproductive. Just like we said in the previous chapter that we are a product of our thoughts, in like manner, we are a product of our habits. What we repeatedly think or do each day shapes our personalities and our lives. I love the way Mahatma Gandhi puts it. He said,

"Your beliefs become your thoughts,
your thoughts become your words,
your words become your actions,
your actions become your habits,
your habits become your values,
your values become your destiny".

You may be asking, "Why does she sweep every night before bed, and is this healthy or unhealthy? My response is yes, it is healthy for me because of the following: Firstly, cleaning is therapeutic for me. Secondly, it saves me time especially as I do it when the kids are in bed. Thirdly, waking up to a cleaned and organised environment is a comforting, refreshing, and motivating way to start my day. So, my cleaning habit is a gain for me. However, if at any point I realised it's no longer healthy, I will need to change my routine. In our journey from surviving to thriving or to turning our pain into gain, our habits become a fundamental element which we cannot ignore. We need to be willing to alter our ways of operating to achieve different and beneficial results. But before we attempt doing so, we need to re-visit the roots of our habits.

Where do habits come from and how are they formed?

I am sure by now you know the first answer – of course, from our parents, culture, growth environment, the media, friends, institutional policies and from our willingness to achieve our dreams in life. If you were raised in a home with parents who smoke, for example, you might develop a smoking habit. Likewise, when we hang out with friends who drink excessively, we may also develop a drinking habit. We also can't forget our cultures or workplaces, where we are conditioned to behave in a certain way for specific reasons.

The response to the second question is simple because habits are formed through repetition. Charles Duhiggs, in his book *The Power of Habit,* explains that habits start with a psychological pattern called a "habit loop", which has three processes – the cue or trigger which tells your brain to perform a behaviour, the behaviour itself, and the reward, which is something that the brain loves, and as such, would always remind you to perform that behaviour again. Unfortunately, although one's brain may enjoy the reward, which is usually temporary, the long-term result could be damaging to one's mental and physical self and life's aspirations. For instance, the brain could enjoy eating that chocolate bar, especially as happy chemicals like serotonin are released, but unhealthy levels of consumption may lead to long-term health problems (weight gain, diabetes, heart problems). Hence, we need to pay attention to the results of our habits to determine the rewards. A healthy mind and body can lead to gain, while an unhealthy mind and body may lead to pain.

When I began my recovery journey, I questioned all the habits I had built over the years, the people who contributed to my habits as well as the environment and culture. I questioned whether each of my habits builds me or breaks me. The outcome of this exercise was transformative because I ditched my unproductive habits and created productive ones. For instance, I changed my people-pleasing habit to creating assertiveness and saying "No" as needed. I also changed my poor habit of eating sugary foods, to eating more fruits and vegetables. I must confess that these new habits have become my lifestyle and have benefited my mental and physical health, my relationships, and my goals.

That might also be a question to ask yourself – Is this unhealthy eating, smoking and drinking, making or breaking me? Is this aggression, passiveness, lateness, deception, laziness, and untidiness, making or breaking me? And the list can be endless. As a side note: for anyone who is a parent, we must evaluate our habits because our habits, good or bad, are contagious. What we repeatedly do becomes normalised within the home, and these can have immediate, medium, and long-term impacts on our kids. As mentioned, I am sure you won't be surprised that some of your current habits (healthy or unhealthy) were learned from your parents. Your parents could have learned them from your grandparents, who also copied them from your great-grandparents. So, some of these generational habits become a cycle in the family and that is why it's vital to evaluate these behaviours and break the negative cycle it may be producing in our lives.

> **We need to be willing to alter our ways
> of operating to achieve a different and
> beneficial result.**

Everything Seemed Fine!

The only way to explain the power of healthy habits, especially to pain pals, is by sharing experiences. Thus, my story of overcoming my unhealthy habits may empower you to engage in the changes that will build healthy habits and transform your pain into gain. Sharing experiences with pain pals also helps them to empower those around them. This endless chain boosts the pain pals to continue to work harder for healthy habits.

> **Our habits would either charge or drain
> the battery of our mind, rendering it usable
> or useless.**

Before my mental rebirth, the results of my habits remained unproductive, albeit I felt comfortable and convinced that I was on the right path as a very busy lady; full-time employee, wife and mum. I felt happy juggling household chores, two jobs, my husband, kids, church activities and other family demands. With my limiting mindset, I believed that functioning on autopilot was all I needed and each day I became more confident that my thoughts, behaviour, and habits were healthy. But in hindsight, I realised that things were actually falling apart but I was too busy to notice the impact of my habits and other people's habits on my life. I focused on meeting endless goals, unable to ignite my consciousness to make a definite decision and say "enough is enough".

The decision to turn my pain into gain sparked the need to re-evaluate my habits. This is because the only way I could achieve different results was to do things differently. While not all my behaviours were bad, I found that I needed to enhance some and replace others completely. It was also essential to be more conscientious in every decision I made. This wasn't a change that I was creating to benefit others. **It was for me!** Thus, it was necessary to take charge of my thoughts, emotions and actions every day, to account for every second, minute and hour of my time, and to track my habits, gauging the results they were producing and ensuring they aligned with my desired goals. I meant business!

One morning, I returned home after I dropped off my kids in school and began reflecting. I switched off my phone and asked myself what the problem was. I repeatedly asked, "What is the problem?" This led me to ponder on the following:

- What could be the cause of my broken relationship in spite of my hard work, being a full-time staff member, loving wife and mum?
- What could be the cause of my financial crisis even though I had two jobs? Why could I not boast of 1000 pounds' savings?
- Why was I so ignorant about life and relationship matters in spite of having a master's degree?

- Why was I emotionally lonely even though I had a family and was always busy?
- Why did I lack the confidence and courage to start my business and achieve my dreams?

As a first step, I conducted a self-analysis to identify areas in my habits and behaviours that needed improvement – *"my improvement areas"*. I identified 15 *improving areas* which I believed were the problems. Amongst them were:

- My unwillingness to ask for help
- Poor financial management
- Poor time management
- Poor networking
- Low self-esteem and passiveness
- Poor planning and Reflection
- People-Pleasing
- Easily trusting and forgiving
- Lacking assertiveness
- Poor communication skill
- Little or no quality time with myself

I began by identifying my improvement areas because I held strongly that I had to enhance or replace the daily unhealthy habits that sustained these flaws. If you look at the list, you will think that some of them are strengths, especially my unwillingness to ask for help. However, as much as I enjoyed doing stuff on my own and not relying on people, it was emotionally and physically draining. It was essential for me to understand that it was fine to ask for help when necessary, and to do so in the right way. I realised that it was common for people to take advantage of my strengths and weaknesses because each time I showed a willingness to do everything, they would cunningly abandon their duties to me. As a result, I found myself always trying to keep the status quo, especially in my relationship. I also realised that some people lacked common sense in relationships, and I learned not to assume that they understood their duties. Hence, I learned to tell people what I needed from them and to seek help appropriately.

As a second step, I came up with options that could enhance each *improvement area* which led me to the following:

- **Poor financial management**: I said, I will:
  - Save a minimum of 10% of my wages each month.
  - Not buy what I don't need.
  - Set a monthly spending cap.
  - Always check my pantry, wardrobe and make a shopping list before I step into any shop.
  - Keep track of my spending each month.
- **People-Pleasing:** I said, I will:
  - **STOP** trying to please people.
  - Not accept doing what I can't do.
  - Learn to say no, without feeling guilty.
  - Ask people to give me space and some time to reflect before responding to their request.
- **Poor Communication Skills:** I said, I will:
  - Read at least one book each month.
  - Watch one YouTube video on communication each day.
  - Pay attention to non-verbal communication.

- Always listen to myself when I talk.
- Speak up whenever I need to, without being scared.
- Be honest, assertive and objective.
- Not speak if I don't have to.
- Actively listen during conversations.

It took me a few days to complete each *improvement area,* and the aim was to create alternative ways of achieving different results, which I integrated into my goals as we will discuss in Chapter 13. At first, I found it challenging to come up with options, but thank goodness for having Google. For example, I googled "How to improve communication skills", read self-help books, and watched YouTube videos. Aren't we lucky to be living in this information age? This is an era where, with a click on our gadgets, we can get answers to every problem.

The final step was to introduce these action points into my daily routine, which has drastically transformed my life. It has improved my confidence, the relationship with myself and others, and enabled me to uncover my passion and purpose, with a clear direction to achieving my dreams. As *Pain Candidates,* how we begin our day has a massive impact on how the rest of the day unfolds. Creating a morning or daily routine is not about trying to live like a robot or being compelled to function by the books and check-off boxes. Instead, it is about allowing yourself to command your morning and your day; to create positive emotions like gratitude, optimism, and courage, which can aid you in beginning your day with a positive attitude. Just to give you a snapshot of my current daily routine; my alarm goes off at 6 am Monday – Friday, and my schedule is as follows:

Morning Routine
- From 6 – 6:30 am, I meditate/pray and do my positive affirmations
- 6:30 – 7 am, I read a book
- 7 - 7:30 am, I exercise
- 7:30 – 8:45 am, I prepare myself and kids, have breakfast and drop off at school.

Mid-Morning and Afternoon Routine
- I go to work or do volunteering or personal development training
- I pick up kids and prepare dinner
- In between these activities, I watch YouTube videos on personal development.

Maybe you're like the old me, who used to either jump out of bed and off, I am gone; or the old me who would hit the snooze button until I was finally late for work; or maybe you're the old me that never bothered about breakfast or engaging in some mindfulness. Oh! One more thing: - What about always checking social media platforms for trending news and gossips, or worrying about what happened the previous day? In a nutshell, I had no Gainful or Productive morning routine. No wonder I was functioning on autopilot, not achieving my goals, not organised enough, not mentally and physically healthy, and trapped in low self-confidence.

Going through these steps was an eye-opener and a transformation for me because of the following: Firstly, the new mindset was completely different from my previous mindset, and for the first time, I could gauge my performance and productivity. Secondly, this new mentality had a positive impact on my kids, especially my daughter. At the time, I shared my bedroom with my daughter, and each time I woke up to begin my daily routine, she would also. She, too, was struggling with her self-confidence and irrational beliefs, and in the process, my *mental rebirth* became infectious. She developed an interest in reading self-help books, especially business books, which has now become an integral element of her life. With a new mindset, she is now encouraging her friends to do the same. In retrospect, I can only imagine what would have happened to my kids and me, if I didn't make that decision to turn my pain into gain. Lastly, I was also awakened to the fact that something had changed. I realised that the focus was on me and not on others. I also noticed that I could finally stay on track and achieve my goals. Do I stringently follow this daily routine? My answer is No, especially during my early days of creating the routine. Sometimes, I miss out on reading a book or exercising or going to bed on time. But whenever that happens, I wilfully and immediately get back on track. Just like any other habit which is formed through repetition, this routine has become my lifestyle. Thus, creating a structured routine will facilitate our success.

The journey of Pain to Gain is to change you, and nobody else.

Something Changed

How many times have you created routines like these, which never worked? I have done it countless times, and they all eventually died a natural death. Hence, this wasn't my first and wouldn't be my last. You will agree with me that creating healthy habits like these is not usually a daunting task. A common example is what most of us do on the 31st of every December, right? We always list the Dos and Don'ts in our New Year's resolutions. I used to be a pro in this activity which seldomly gets implemented. After all, I wasn't alone. According to U.S News & World Report, the failure rate for new year's resolutions is said to be about 80%, and most people lose their resolve by February. Does that come as a surprise? In my opinion, the problem is not with the creation, but with the implementation.

When I read these statistics, I was curious to understand the reason for such a massive failure. There are many personal reasons, some of which are: lack of clarity, lack of time, demotivation, lack of confidence, too much hurry, too ambitious, pressure, wrong motive, wrong method, lack of resources, resistance to change, and the list goes on. However, after conducting my self-examination, the three most important reasons to me are what I called:

THE 3 Ms

- **Motive/Motivation:** Why do you want a new habit?
- **Method:** How are you going to achieve it?
- **Maintenance:** How are you going to maintain it?

In my view, these are the three crucial questions and determinants for creating healthy or successful and lasting habits. Whenever I ask my *pain pals* their reasons for wanting to form new healthy habits, I notice that many do so for the wrong reasons. And in retrospect, I also used to create routines just to please others. No wonder I struggled! We would usually have rationales like:

- Because my partner said so.
- Because the Doctor says so.
- Because my work wants it.
- Because my friends demand it.
- Because of that competition.
- Because I want to prove a point.
- Because I need it for such and such an occasion.

While these reasons could be valid, sadly, they are external motivators, meaning, they emanate from others, not from you and I, and seek to satisfy others. In other words, if we had our way, we wouldn't be bothered to engage in any such healthy habits. Nevertheless, some of these external motivators may indeed persuade us to create and implement beneficial habits, which can enable us to achieve a desired reward or purpose. A doctor, for example, might want a patient to stop smoking due to the high risk of lung disease. If the patient complies and successfully quits smoking, the lesser chance of developing lung disease would be the patient's reward for quitting. But how many of us fail to heed the professional's recommendations, even when we know it's for our good? That's when we make statements like, "My Doctor says

I should reduce my alcohol intake, but I'm not bothered." We're not usually bothered because we focus on the external, rather than the internal persuader. So, I would say the best incentive for a successful practice needs to come from within you – internally motivated. Before you think of creating any new productive habit, you should have evaluated the benefits that it gives **you** and **you** alone. Nevertheless, we can also have a combination of external and internal motivators. Your partner, for example, may indeed want you to lose weight and would accompany you to the gym each time. But what are the benefits of losing weight to you? How would you feel when you successfully lost weight? Do you value the benefits? If so, in what ways?

As *Pain Candidates,* providing genuine answers to these questions becomes an anchor to creating, implementing, and maintaining a healthy or thriving habit. If you value the benefits of a new gainful routine, you will also believe in it and be confident that you can achieve it. Therefore, each time you think about the reward it brings to your wellbeing, you'll be highly inspired to keep going, and your desire for the reward that comes with those healthy habits will soar.

I must also add that sometimes we're good at working under pressure because we want to please others. If that is you, you may still succeed in the creation and implementation of a successful habit, but not the maintenance; especially once you have pleased the external motivators. For example, maybe you needed a new healthy eating habit just to fit into that wedding dress. Once the wedding ceremony is over, you could slip back into your old routine, except you value the benefits of a slimmer body. In this case, the confidence and health benefits might motivate you to maintain your new healthy eating habit.

2nd M - Method

The next factor or the 2nd M is the Method. Again, sometimes, we fail because of wrong methodology of executing the new routine. When we create a new routine, we are usually so excited and eager to see an over-night result. That is why Gyms are usually packed in the 1st and 2nd weeks of January. For many, if they do not achieve a certain target at a certain time, they become discouraged. This is especially if they are doing it just to please others. We seem to forget that successfully forming a new healthy habit takes time, particularly changing a prolonged unhealthy habit.

In my view, the key to a successful healthy habit is to take tiny and consistent steps each day, week, or month. Rather than take a giant leap, get exhausted and take a break, it is more rewarding to make small and steady steps. For example, if you used to consume 20 custard cream biscuits a day, try reducing it to 18. From there, you decrease to 17, 16, 15 and so forth, until you get to one or none a day! We need to sacrifice specific thoughts, behaviours and favourites to achieve the positive results we desire in life.

3rd M – Maintenance

The last M is Maintenance. Another key to forming a successful habit is the ability to maintain it. This element is very crucial, especially for my *pain pals or even you, the reader.* Why do we quickly regress to old habits or distorted thought patterns?

There seem to be many reasons why people often relapse from their commitments and the most common are psychological. While the reasons remain unique, they are either a deviation from primary motives or poor methodological application. When we quickly regress to our old habits, for example, it is usually a deviation from the motive and method, which may have been triggered by an event. In other words, two things can affect our commitment to sustain a new habit and achieve our required results. Firstly, it is when we no longer value the benefits or believe in why we do what we do. Secondly, when we drastically change the method we initially applied, this might affect our progress.

This explanation can be understood by sharing with you the experience of Rachel (my pain pal). I cultivated a habit of always checking on my *pain pals*, to keep them motivated. From the progress that Rachel had made with her new healthy habits, I was confident that she had taken back control of her wellbeing. I could tell she was pleased with her life. She had relocated to a safer environment, started a part-time job, had a quality relationship with herself and her kids, sorted childcare, was dating again and had also enrolled in a college course. Everything seemed to be going well for her. We didn't communicate for three weeks, and when I called her, she was at the lowest point of her life. She was stressed and less motivated for anything. When I asked her why she had relapsed, she couldn't figure out the cause. I felt her emotional pain and was curious to understand more because that would help me to support her effectively. After a deep breath, she said, "It's my fault. I had thought that going to college was the best thing for me to boost my self-esteem, gain a qualification and get my dream job (nursing). But I don't think this is the right time for me. I just started the course and couldn't handle the pressure…"

I understood that although her motive was still intact, the method for maintaining her current healthy habits had shifted due to her commencing the college course. So, starting her college course needed her to create a new routine, which seemed strenuous for her. I also noticed that inconsistency in one habit might upset the others. Starting college required Rachel to sleep late and wake up earlier than usual. She needed to be in college on time, study and submit her assignments, which was hectic for her and caused her to relapse. Thus, whenever the motive or the method changes, it could easily affect the maintenance.

The motives and methods for forming new healthy habits can always be reviewed when circumstances change, and Rachel needed to adjust her current routines to incorporate her college course in a realistic and achievable manner. Besides, she needed to ensure that her current routine was realistic and achievable. Moreover, she needed to pay attention to the internal reward (her confidence, self-esteem, wellbeing, qualification, dream career, better life, etc.). The reward she would get from waking up in the night to study and do her assignments, or waking up early to prepare her kids before going to college would be fulfilling and would remain as her motivations for creating the required healthy habit.

Forming a thriving habit will also require you to evaluate if it is something you can achieve. Is it realistic and achievable? You can't say you want to save £200 a month when you can only afford £100. I understand that sometimes we may be quite ambitious about our goals, but we don't want a goal that will be futile from the start. Once your routine is set, you will develop a unique strategy that will keep you going. As someone who was craving to turn my painful habits into productive habits, all I needed as motivation was my change word and a mental image for the reward I was expecting.

Choosing a Change Word

One trick that I used to resist the temptation of relenting on my new healthy habits was to choose my 'change word'. The word I picked was 'Thriving'. This word was a bedrock to all I wanted. It meant everything – confidence, rational thinking, self-esteem, happiness, time management, quality relationships, financial management, etc. Each time I said, "thriving", it ignited excitement and the willingness to implement my healthy routines. Also, whenever I felt distracted, the word would redirect my focus on my anticipated rewards, forcing me to stay on track. My change word was like a wheel, rolling me along to my desired destination. Of course, my inner voice tried its luck. It gave me all the reasons why I could not achieve the results I was seeking. But I resisted! In addition, I was intentional and alert with anything I did or said. If I unconsciously labelled myself as "stupid", for example, I would immediately correct myself. The experience was like being on an internship, the only difference being that I was the trainee and the trainer. Before time, I started noticing some changes in my habits and the positive results I was getting. My greatest joy was always at the end of the day when I took stock of how I had spent my day. I accounted for every hour I used, and that was a way of tracking my progress., I asked myself questions, rated on a scale of 1-10, like:

- How well did you do today?
- What was the ratio of your positive thoughts to negative thoughts?
- How many new words did you learn today? (just one was enough)
- How gentle were you today to yourself and others?
- How assertive were you today in your conversations?
- What lessons did you learn today?

My ratings gave me further impetus to do well the next day. I know this may sound too much, but **when you genuinely need a change in your life, you will go to any length to achieve that change.** I did precisely that, and this book is a testament to the result I achieved. I am confident that you, too, can accomplish your dreams.

One factor that tends to limit our abilities to create and maintain healthy habits is often our inability to let go of our unhealthy habits (thoughts, emotions, behaviours). Choosing to relinquish is like choosing to empty a dirty bottle, before refilling it with clean water. Trying to hold on to the dirty fluid prevents us from having the opportunity of a new replacement. Many pain candidates may know **why** we need to let go, but we do not know **how** to let go, which will be the focus of our next chapter.

When you genuinely need a change in your life, you will go to any length to achieve that change.

CHAPTER 8

Step 6: Relinquish/ Let Go

Letting go is not a favour done to others,
but a blessing done to you

Okay, let's play would you rather.

1. Would you rather keep your current phone, or dispose of it and get a new one for free?
2. Would you rather accept £500 now, or get £1000 tomorrow?
3. Would you rather keep an old nagging friend, or have no friend?
4. Would you rather survive or thrive?

Well done for playing! There's no right or wrong answer; it all depends on your preferences and experiences. Based on a painful experience, for example, I may rather accept £500 now than wait for £1000 tomorrow because I might never get it. On the other hand, I may choose to take the risk and be £500 richer the next day. It all comes down to making a choice. As adults, some of the decisions we make in life could leave us with good or bad memories. We have memories of hurtful experiences caused by events and people in the form of betrayals, physical and emotional abuse, a series of bad luck, illnesses, deaths of loved ones and our human errors. And from time to time, we cannot help but think about the past. In this chapter, we shall be referring to '**our painful past**' as those memories that suck our energy, time, and aspirations in life.

For many *Pain Candidates*, each time we approach a specific place, season, date and event, listen to a song, watch a TV program and look at a picture of body scars, it triggers the remembrance of something or someone, and also generates varied emotions. The problem is not about the past because, as humans, we will ALWAYS have one. The problem is whether we allow the thoughts of our painful past to drown our emotions. In other words, when those memories come to mind, what happens from then? Do we brush them off or allow them to wreck our feelings and behaviours?

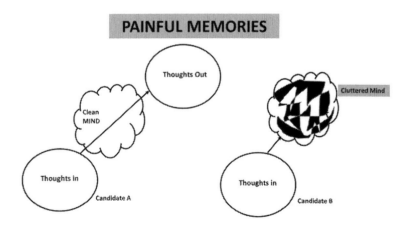

As seen in the picture, candidate **A** has a clear mind because the memories "fly in and out". But candidate **B** has a cluttered mind because they decide to accommodate the memories (which would usually be distorted) and allow it to affect their emotions and behaviours. I must say, it's not that easy to dispel memories of our painful past and have a clear mind like candidate **A**. However, it is possible when we decide to focus on the Gain, rather than the Pain. This is the little secret that helped me overcome the memory of losing my granny which had troubled me for years. As illustrated by the images above, do you identify with candidate A or B? Or could you be any of them depending on the circumstance?

My Weeping Episodes

Before my *mental rebirth*, the 11th of March always evoked one of my painful experiences; the day I lost my granny. She was a devoted parishioner and a member of the Catholic Women's Association. After her death, each time I went to church or saw any lady wearing the association's uniform, my pain of losing her kicked in, and it would leave me depressed for days.

For many years, I was troubled with questions like, "Did my birth and poor health contribute to granny's health condition?" "Did she develop liver cancer because she focused on me and forgot about herself?" "Could I have done something more for her?" All these questions aroused feelings of guilt, anger and bitterness against me and for others. I blamed my dad and mum for not being there for me. I also blamed the medical doctors for not doing enough to save granny's life. So, the pain of guilt and bitterness has always been hovering over me, causing me to grieve continually.

It was apparent that these memories were wrecking me emotionally, and the underlying reason was that I had not forgiven myself and others. Secondly, I had not sensibly seen my granny's death as a blessing to me. I was more focused on what did not happen, rather than on what happened – the good memories we shared, the values she taught me, the many faith-filled words she blessed me with, her sacrifices and even the words she spoke in her heart before dying. It is apparent that we concentrate more on the bad than the good and my situation might have triggered your thoughts of hurtful feelings. Maybe right now you can't stop thinking about that failed relationship; the best friend that betrayed you; the family that rejected you; the loved one you lost; the job you lost; the business that failed, and how you even messed up. Nevertheless, what about the good times you shared? What about the lessons you learned? When I reflected on all of these, I couldn't help but repeat the words of apostle Paul who said,

> *"I have fought the good fight of faith, I have finished the race, I have kept the faith. Now there is in store for me the crown of righteousness, which the Lord, the righteous Judge, will award to me on that day – and not only to me, but also to all who have longed for his appearance."* (2 Timothy 4:7-8)

After reflecting on this statement, I said to myself, "Yes! Granny fought a good fight." This book is the benefit of the good fight. Instead of dreading the month of March, I now celebrate it! It reminds me that I have come too far to tolerate my painful past sinking my life. And to think of it, Granny would be most happy to see me thriving in life; it satisfies her soul that she didn't fight in vain. With this mindset, I have consciously decided to let go of the guilt or any lack of forgiveness. Are there any such negative emotions holding you back?

Forgiveness

Speaking with my *pain pals*, the impression I gather is that forgiveness is only for religious people. That is not true! Anyone can exercise their right to forgive or let go of their painful past. Forgiveness, however, needs to begin with you. It is vital you forgive yourself first and refuse to be pinned down by guilt. Remember, we said in Chapter Six that when a painful event occurs, we could either blame or criticise ourselves or others for the negative results. So, blame or criticism accompanies guilt. But once you forgive yourself, you can easily forgive others. Psychologists generally define forgiveness as:

> "A conscious, deliberate decision to release feelings of resentment or vengeance towards someone who harmed or hurt you, regardless of whether they actually deserve your forgiveness".

Will Meek (a counselling psychologist) in an article in *Psychology Today*, mentions that Forgiveness DOES NOT mean the following:

- That what happened was ok - we are not condoning or tolerating pain or harmful behaviours.

- That if I forgive, it might happen to me again - we shouldn't hang on to the negative emotions as a defence mechanism.
- That I should immediately forget the physical or emotional scars I incurred as a result of the painful experience. (Healing takes time, but faster if your mind is at peace).
- That I should return to any painful or abusive relationship.
- That I will become a bad person if I don't forgive (We shouldn't be pressured to forgive; it is a choice).

To these, I add that forgiveness does not mean we should take matters into our hands and disrupt any ongoing legal process. There is a justice system that punishes those who violate the law and that has got nothing to do with you and me; we did not set those laws. Thus, if an offender violates the law, and is deemed to pose a threat to the public, we cannot prevent the law from being enforced. Also, dropping a charge against someone is voluntary. Forgiveness means, releasing any feeling of bitterness against someone and genuinely wishing that they could learn in the process of it and change for the better. I can only hope that offenders can ignite their consciousness to the damage caused by their behaviour; take responsibility for their actions; find their real purpose in life; change their thinking pattern; create healthy habits and let go of their damaging behaviours.

**It is vital you forgive yourself first and refuse
to be pinned down by guilt.**

The Pain of Not Letting Go

Have you decided to write your painful past on the sand or engraved it on marble? Those who write it on the sand easily let it go. But those who engraved it on marble, hold on to it for the rest of their lives. They allow those painful pasts to interfere with their present decisions, which affect their future. Our past has come and gone! We cannot undo it. Although we may allow the past to dominate our present, that still doesn't change the fact that it's the past. It is also true that the consequences could still be affecting us now. However, we must decide on how to move on to a better future. Remember that the past is gone, and we do not know what the future brings, but we have the **'present'**, which is a gift that we can use to determine our future. Hence, if we keep on clinging on to the past, we may ruin our future. As mentioned, the key to turning your pain to gain applies knowledge and experiences from a painful past to anticipate a gainful future. Otherwise, our past will hold us HOSTAGE, which, as an acronym, defines the effects of our negative past on ourselves and our environment as follows:

H - Health
O - Others
S – Self-Image
T – Time
A – Aspirations
G - Growth
E – Energy

H - Health

We cannot emphasise enough how our negative thinking or beliefs damage our mental and physical health. When we hold onto the negative experiences, they create negative feelings of resentment, anger, revenge, fear, guilt, anxiety and depression. Think of how you feel each time you dwell on that painful past. Does it make or break your health? How long have you been holding your health hostage? **It's time to let go.**

O - Others

The quality of our lives depends on the quality of our relationships, which includes the relationship with ourselves and our thoughts. Because no one can live an isolated life, we need to form healthy relationships and interact with people, whether at home, work, college, events and even on the streets. But when our relationships lead us to constant complaining, recounting past painful stories, blaming others, blaming ourselves and being consistently negative, people may begin to isolate us. Our partner, kids, friends, colleagues and even strangers could start avoiding us. Nobody wants to be around someone with constant toxic behaviour. And when this happens, loneliness might kick in which only further affects our lives. Think about the damage you may have caused in your relationships, just because you kept holding on to the past. How many times have you likened your partner, kids, friends and family members to someone that hurt you in the past? Does this build or destroy your rapport? How long would you allow it to hold your relationships and social life hostage? **It is time to let it go.**

S - Self-esteem

Maxwell Maltz said, *"Low self-esteem is like driving through life with your handbrake on."* Having experienced it, I strongly agree that our low self-esteem may inhibit our progress in life. Dwelling on our painful past, the negative labelling and our mistakes cause further damage to our self-esteem. Just because someone called you fat, ugly, stupid, useless and incompetent, doesn't make you so. Again, just because you went off course doesn't mean you can't get back on course. But if you continue to dwell on the pain, you could block your success. Also, when you don't value yourself and believe in your abilities, you lose self-confidence. This feeling holds your life hostage.

T - Time

When we dwell on the past, we waste our precious time. For anyone who has a busy life, 24 hours doesn't seem enough, and we can't afford to lose a single minute. While some people may seem to have all the time, they may not use it efficiently. For those struggling to bounce back after a fall, time is seemingly not on our side. For instance, the time you take to make baseless complaints, replay failed or hurtful scenarios, explain yourself, feel depressed, etc., that time could have been used to achieve something useful. I look at it this way: I only have today to boast of because I might not see tomorrow. People have left their homes for work and never returned. Therefore, life is too short to focus on a painful past and that's why we need to value each second, minute and day. If today was your last day on earth, would you waste it dwelling on your painful past?

A – Aspirations

Many dreams have been killed because of people living in their past. As indicated, If I didn't choose to embark on this journey of turning my pain into gain, my dreams would have been killed. Ideas (great or small) can only be nurtured in a healthy mind. When you're disturbed all the time and incapable of taking charge of your thinking, you choke or prevent your dreams from coming true. I have heard someone tell me that, "my dream is to fall in love with a loving and caring man and walk down the aisle", yet she doesn't want to let go of the one that broke her heart. It is necessary to empty a dirty bottle before it can be refilled with clean water. So, we do not need to allow our past to define our future. Take the lessons learned from your past and run with it – Just let it go!

G - Growth

We can't grow personally, professionally, financially, and spiritually if we keep dwelling on the past. When I got on my *mental rebirth* journey, I decided not to focus on my painful past. I did not want to dwell on my inherited limiting beliefs, betrayals, mistakes, or the weaknesses and wickedness of others. I was ready to burn all the painful bridges behind me and start anew. I am delighted that the growth and success gained within the years have exceeded that of my whole life combined. That is the magic of letting go.

E - Energy

In my experience, nothing sucks energy from the body like recounting m traumatic experiences. For anyone who has experienced a relationship breakup, I am sure you've witnessed it when family members and friends rang up to sympathise with you, but also wanted to know your side of the story. And for some reason, we always explained ourselves, especially if the other partner's story sounded louder and more acceptable although it wasn't true. I didn't like the experience, and I realised that it wasn't helping me; nor was it changing anything. As a result, I decided that I wouldn't waste my time explaining myself to anybody. People could believe whatever they thought about me, but I didn't care. This decision brought peace and revived my energy. As *Pain Candidates*, when we lack power, it reduces our ability to focus or stay productive.

It is worth noting that these elements (H.O.S.T.A.G.E) are intertwined. An unhealthy mind or body, for example, can affect your relationship with others, your aspirations, growth, self-esteem, time and energy. So, it is crucial to keep checks and balances on each of these areas. Refuse to let your past hold you hostage and turn your Painful past into a Gainful future.

The key to turning your pain into gain is to use the knowledge and experiences learned from your past, to create a Gainful future for you.

How to Let Go of the Past

Have you noticed that it's usually easy to tell people to "let go" or "just forgive"? Letting go of our painful past is not as easy as it may sound. For someone who experienced the pain nearly all of their life or who has been gravely affected, the pain becomes their 'identity or DNA'. It can be hard to separate the two. If this is you, you don't need to deal with it alone. You need to understand that it is not taboo to be experiencing what you are going through. As we shared in Chapter Six, it is ok to speak up - seek professional help or share the pain with someone whom you trust. Reading self-help books like this one and seeking tailored therapy could help. As a *Pain Candidate* like you, I let go of my painful past by applying **GRATITUDE.**

G – Grateful
R – Re-assess
A – Accept
T – Talk
I – Itemised
T – Trash
U – Uncover
D – Dive in
E – Enjoy

G - Grateful

My first step to recovery was letting go of my painful past and being grateful for being alive. It is a blessing to be counted amongst the living. Yes, I might have lost everything and had to start life all over again, but I was lucky to be alive because others have died in the pain process. Secondly, I was grateful for all that had happened in my life because I conquered all odds to become my own hero. I was also thankful for everyone that crossed my path and all the lessons their kindness and wickedness taught me. In addition, I was grateful for being a mum of three brilliant kids and having family members and friends who love me. Besides, I was thankful that I had finally found my purpose in life, and I still had the opportunity to rewrite my story. So, I was, and I am, **Very Grateful**. Despite all the pain you have been through, is there anything you're still thankful for? Write them down, and you'll be surprised how blessed and worthy you are.

R - Re-assess

My gratitude list inspired me to reassess my painful past and my beliefs or perception towards each event. I asked questions like: "Was that really what I thought? Was it worse than those of others? Were people's actions or omissions intentional? What were the circumstances at the time? If I were in their shoes, would I have acted differently?" Some of these questions began to release the resentment I had towards those who had hurt me. I realised that most of them acted out of good faith notwithstanding the outcomes. For example, after having a talk with my mum, her decision to leave me with my granny was intended to save my life. She also went through traumatic experiences as a 'woman', escaping from obnoxious cultural practices. After assessing her bravery, I can't help but say, "Thank you, Mum, for taking that tough decision to leave me with Granny".

A - Accept.

When my relationship broke up, I was in denial. I couldn't believe that my marriage of over 12 years had come to an end. In my mind, I knew that there were still possibilities for us to resolve our differences and come to a compromise. I tried everything to prove that I wasn't bitter and was always open to reconciliation. But the more I tried, the more I was hurting; until I finally accepted that the relationship was over. That is when I also decided to let go and move on. So, if that is you, you need to accept the reality. It is real! it happened and that's all part of life! Yes, you also need to move on. You are your rescuer.

T - Talk

Haven't you bottled it up for too long? It is time to talk about it. Share with someone or seek professional help. You can also have constant dialogue with yourself. This is one of the techniques that helped me. I used to stand in front of the mirror and address myself. I would use my voice to comfort myself, reassuring me that, "All will be fine". I promised myself that I was going to make me proud, and I did! Don't be ashamed of who you are. You can still bounce back and live a thriving life.

I - Itemised

Sometimes we go through many experiences, with varied emotions, and may be unable to decipher the exact feeling. What I did is that, under each painful experience, I named the person that hurt me, the exact reason why I was angry or hurting, and my decision for letting it go. For example, "I am angry with my parents because… From this day henceforth, I choose to let go of my feeling of bitterness against them…". "I am angry with my partner because…From this day henceforth, I choose to let go of the feeling of bitterness and disappointment against him …" It took me two weeks to let everything and everyone off my chest in writing. That was excellent therapy. Every time I completed each area of pain, I felt a greater sense of peace of mind. Have you got many things bugging your mind? Who are you angry with and why? Try writing them down. Go wild on your sheet of paper – pour out your heart and experience the serenity of your mind.

T - Trash

After I had poured out my mind in writing, I trashed the sheets. You may even want to burn them or bury them somewhere; whichever you choose, it still does the job. When I was trashing mine, I said, "As I trash this pain, I promise from today henceforth never to dwell on them. If ever I speak about it, it shall only be from the standpoint of strength." That was like swearing an oath to myself, which, in a way, worked because I had to keep to the terms.

U - Uncover

Now that the past is come and gone, I needed to embrace the future. It was necessary to uncover the beauty that life has in store for me. I needed to break free from the shackles of my painful past, to discover the real me, uncover my potentials, abilities, and dreams, and embrace more pleasures and adventures. I also needed to uncover new and positive friends. What is it that you need to discover? You must go for it!

D - Dive in

As *Pain Candidates,* once we start uncovering and enjoying all areas of our lives, we realise how our past had held us hostage. As soon as I was confident with myself and my abilities, I needed new experiences. It was vital to dive into new relationships, new adventures, new dreams, new life, new me and new memories. I refused to let my past define me, and I finally succeeded in rewriting my story. Are you willing to dive into the life you were born to live? Are you willing to rewrite your story? If yes, then I can guarantee you will enjoy it!

E - Enjoy

When you finally succeed to turn your pain into gain, all you can do is enjoy your life as it was supposed to be! However, you need some quality people around you to make the journey memorable, that's why we focus on the next step, which is relationships. What is life without quality relationships?

It is a blessing to be counted amongst the living.

CHAPTER 9

Step 7: Interrelation/Relationship

*"As you go out in search for a good life,
go search for People, not wealth."*
- Susan Changsen

Imagine a life or a world without people. Imagine that you had no family member to talk to. Imagine you had no friends, colleagues, customers, business associates or health professionals.

In my view, human existence and relationship is the only reason why we were born and why we live. We live to serve people and to be served by people. Nobody is or can be an island because we are intrinsically a social species. We also interrelate with each other and humanity flourishes on relationships. Dr Seligman

"Alone I can 'Say' but together we can 'Talk'. Alone I can 'Enjoy' but together we can 'Celebrate'.

Alone I can 'Smile' but together we can 'Laugh'. That's the BEAUTY of Human Relationships. We're nothing without each other."

- quoteshwar.com

in his book – *Flourish,* outlines human connection as one of the six elements of happiness and wellbeing, with which I strongly agree. In my view, we also can't enjoy a thriving life without thriving relationships.

I began with a quote from my granny which she would often use as a farewell whenever a family member was leaving home in search of a better life. In her view, money can indeed buy everything, but it takes people to create and deliver that "everything". As an exhortation, she would always stress the need to search for people and not wealth and that message has always stuck with me. It is always comforting to know that I have someone to count on for needed support.

In as much as relationships can be rewarding, some can also be exploitative depending on the personalities of those we associate with. Hence, in our pain to gain journey, we need to pay attention to our relationships. The question I always ask is: "Is this relationship a Negative or a Plus?" A negative relationship is the kind that sucks or drains your time, energy, peace, happiness, money, dreams, and your life. In this kind of relationship, each time you meet the person or group of persons, you are bound to leave in a 'negative'. This is because something has been taken out of you, with no equivalent benefit to you. On the other hand, a Plus relationship is nurturing and productive. In this kind of relationship, you feel valued, loved, comfortable, refreshed, encouraged, and empowered.

Unfortunately, we live in a highly technological, materialistic, and judgmental world; a world where the value of human relationships seems to have diminished. Our relationships appear to have no depth of quality; hence pain becomes inevitable, especially the pain of loneliness. According to statistics, loneliness is seen as one of the most significant health concerns we face today.[6] The reason I picked on loneliness is that this is one of the most neglected agonies that is endured by *Pain Candidates*. The hypercritical attitude of people in our circles kills the love and confidence we have for ourselves and others. As a result, we may struggle to create and maintain relationships because of the fear of societal views.

During my *mental rebirth* journey, I realised that if I was serious about turning my pain into gain, then I had to be serious about sorting out my relationships. And this meant evaluating, and categorising my relationships; were my existing relationships making or breaking me? I was ready to focus my time and energy more on building a few quality relationships that would last a lifetime, than having many shallow ones that do not serve me. This prompted me to create my relationship hierarchy because I needed to be accountable for the time and energy given to each relationship and the accompanying benefits.

Whatever relationship you have right now should be adding and not subtracting value from your life.

Relationship Hierarchy

How worthy and deep are your relationships?

I wish someone had asked me these questions years back. Although I had many relationships in my life (partner, kids,

---

[6] https://www.cdc.gov/aging/publications/features/lonely-older-adults.html

family, friends, colleagues, etc.), I realised I needed more than just "a relationship" - **some prioritisation and depth in my relationships**. In terms of **priority**, I needed to know who came at the top or bottom of my relationship triangle. I asked myself questions like, "What is it that I missed in my relationships? Were my priorities, right?" This reflective exercise wasn't intended to ignite self-blaming or guilt, but to help me in my future relationships. I wanted to extract the lessons learned and use them to create and maintain gainful future relationships.

Regarding **depth**, I focused on the quality of my relationships. How deep is the love, commitment, communication, trust, honesty, transparency, and respect within my relationships? I realised that the depth of each component would depend on the relationship hierarchy. For example, the level of commitment I have for my kids might not be the same as that for my friends. Or the level of transparency I have for my spouse may not be as that for my extended family.

As *pain candidates*, identifying and creating our relationship hierarchy will help us to focus our time and energy where it is due. It will also aid us to strengthen those relationships that are valuable to our spiritual, emotional and physical wellbeing. As a result, I came up with what I termed **"My Relationship Hierarchy"**.

My relationship hierarchy flows from top to bottom in order of priority. Looking at my triangle and its ranking, it could be completely different from yours. Our relationship hierarchy is based on our varied circumstances - personalities, culture, values, social status, priorities, and the like. The idea is to help you to create your personalised triangle and focus on the depth of your relationship.

RELATIONSHIP HIERARCHY

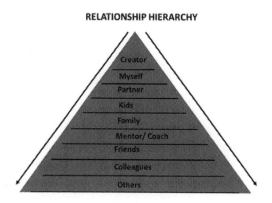

It is also to enable you to devote your time and energy where it is required.

My Creator (God)

The top of my triangle is **God - my creator**. I really don't mind which appellation you may use. Call it God, the universe, source energy, supreme being, and so on. What matters to me is the relationship that exists between me and someone or something higher than me. Although I am a Christian, that doesn't make me more valuable than anyone else. We all have some form of faith or belief, and I respect everyone's view. If we could all choose what resonates with us and embrace everyone's choice, the world would be a more peaceful place. Without going into theories, controversies and debates surrounding the creation of the universe, my only conviction is that I was created and placed on this planet, Earth, by someone. I am 100% convinced, based on my faith and biblical teaching, that there is a God, and he created me. So, my relationship with him is likened to that of a product and its manufacturer.

Only a manufacturer knows the purpose and the value of its product. And unless he makes it known, the product might not be valued as it should. In the same manner, God is the source of my life. The air I breathe comes from him. He alone knows my value and why I was created and placed on this earth. And unless he reveals that purpose to me, I might not value myself; others may not appreciate me, and I might not be living the life that I should.

Myself

In the 2nd position, it is me! Before my *mental rebirth,* I would probably have been at the bottom of the triangle. No wonder I always felt guilty each time I treated myself to anything nice or spent some quality time with myself. Being at the bottom, I was focused on pleasing everyone, empowering, and changing others' mindsets, except mine. I had no time to sit back and reflect on the impact of my lack of self-love. I also didn't realise that I live with myself 24/7, so, I needed to be patient, honest, communicate, value, respect, love, honour, trust and be kind to myself. Today, these virtues now flow from me to those around me. We must understand that we can't give what we don't have, and we may not receive what we can't provide. Choosing to educate and love yourself is the best gift you can give yourself and your loved ones. Education builds self-confidence and enhances our emotional intelligence. And I hope that by the time you finish reading this book, your mindset of yourself will be completely different.

Partner

My partner comes in the 3rd position. If you're a parent, you would probably be saying, "No way! My kids come before my partner." And you know what? You are not alone because statistics show that most women (me included), and some men put their kids first over their spouses. What do you think could be the reason for this? In my viewpoint, this seems to be a parental instinct, especially knowing the vulnerability of our children and our duty to protect them. Being a mother, the desire to put our kids first is beyond human understanding. The journey from yearning for a child, through gestation, labour, delivery and bonding, creates a special place in our hearts for our kids.

No matter the reasons we give for placing our kids first, we must also comprehend that when **living together as a family,** the well-being of our kids depends on the quality of our relationship with our partner. The quality of the relationship with our kids also relies on the quality of our relationship with our partner, meaning that if we are saying that we love our kids, the first evidence is by cherishing our spouse (their mum or dad). This is because a loving relationship provides the foundation for building a healthy family. Besides, our kids feel better, happier, safer, more loved, and educated when both parents are happy. Remember we said in Chapter Seven that behaviours could be contagious? Kids will pick up from the love, reciprocity, respect, teamwork, and communication displayed by both parents. And these are some of the values that they take with them into their relationships.

Kids

Kids (born or adopted) come in 4th place. The reason for being in this position is because I need to give them the best of me. I need to express and demonstrate love, kindness, patience, joy, peace, respect, forgiveness, trust, commitment, and self-control. I cannot show all these without first developing a quality relationship with the first three categories (God, self and partner). We need a physically and emotionally stable mind and body, and to be present and available for our kids. We also want to pass over the positive values that would become a foundation for their relationships and happiness. Thus, it is important to develop a healthy relationship with ourselves and enhance our personal growth, which, in return, can be a gain for our kids.

Family

My family comes in the 5th position on my triangle. This involves my extended family - parents, siblings, and my partner's family. Before my *mental rebirth*, this would have been in the 3rd position. My family is valuable. However, my nuclear family remain as the anchor of my relationship and remains the most important. Again, the quality of my relationship with the extended family might not impact my wellbeing as that of my nuclear family, even though they remain vital and serve as a buffer to our lives.

Mentor

My mentor comes in 6th place. We might have mentors, coaches, counsellors or anyone in a professional capacity who supports us to enhance our wellbeing. Professionals are there to add value to our lives and relationships, especially when we need to make important, but sensitive life decisions. I never appreciated the importance of having a life coach until I began my change journey. My coach is a blessing in my life, and because of our reliability, we have developed an amazing relationship. She pulls me along whenever I feel demoralised, which is what pain pals need. As *Pain Candidates*, I encourage you to look for someone whom you trust and who believes in your abilities, to walk this journey with you.

Friends

My friends come in 7th position. During the peak of my pain, I realised that I didn't have quality or Plus friends as I thought. There are many categories of friends and Geoffrey identifies four types in his book, *Buddy System: Understanding Male Friendships*. These are: **Must friends** - someone who's there for you 24/7 whenever you need them for support. **Trust friends** - someone whom you trust, and who also believes in you. It's also someone who respects you, and you feel comfortable being around them, or someone you're always looking forward to meeting. **Rust friends** - someone whom you've known for a very long time, and there's nothing more you need to get closer to them unless something changes, but they remain a part of your life. **Just friends** - someone you meet or see regularly within your community (in a shop, at your kids' school, GP surgery, local club etc.), whose company you enjoy, but you have no intention or desire of socialising with them or knowing them personally.

All the while, I believed I had Must and Trust friends, only to find out that most of them acted as Rust and Just friends. That is because they were never there for me when I needed them the most. The same friends with whom I shared my pain, treated me scornfully. I am sure you have been in that position where you feel like you have more Painful than Gainful friends.

When I left my relationship, I felt like I was a 'waste'. I also felt 'stupid' to have loved my 'friends' more than they loved me. I believed in them more than they did in me. Moreover, I sacrificed for them more than they did for me. While I don't hate them, I am grateful that their attitudes ignited my self-consciousness and taught me the meaning of true friendship. So, my unpleasant experience with my friends made me focus my time and energy on building relationships other than friendships. However, I have created a new network of positive friends, which I hope will be better than my previous ones. If your friendship network makes you lose confidence, it is better to create another friendship network.

Colleagues

My colleagues come in the 8th position. Although some of my colleagues have become my Trust friends, our relationship is work-based. I have created a quality relationship that promotes teamwork, communication, understanding, respect and increased work productivity. We must create a healthy working relationship at work because it is where we spend a third of our time. We can't afford to be in an environment where it is unconducive and drains our energy - There is no need to have Painful Colleagues. If that sounds like your working environment, you might consider resolving any current issue or looking for other job opportunities.

Once I had prioritised my relationships, the next steps were to improve or delete those that were no longer serving me; alter where my time, energy and money were going and create a level of consistency where love, trust, transparency, communication, honesty, commitment, and respect could be sustained in other areas of priority. For example, I needed to communicate and be more transparent with my partner than my friends or extended family. It was also necessary to deepen the shallow relationships that weren't producing a positive impact on me and those around me. Thanks to this ranking, I have developed a deeper relationship with myself and my kids, and I look forward to developing a deeper relationship with my future partner. I also noticed that when I create a deeper connection with the top six relationships on my triangle, I develop a greater sense of wellbeing or happiness. It is important to mention that priorities change with our changing circumstances. Hence, we can alter our relationship positions as needed. As *Pain Candidates,* we need to understand that it's not the quantity of people we keep in our inner circle, but the quality of the relationship that matters.

**A loving relationship provides the foundation
for building a healthy family. Our kids feel
better, happier, safer, more loved, and educated
when both parents are happy.**

The Gain of Effective Communication

One of the most valuable elements in our relationship is communication. Without it, relationships can't be formed, nurtured or sustained. Whenever there is a breakdown in communication in any relationship, every other aspect of the relationship could be affected. As we know, human relationships are formed by imperfect beings, hence, they are susceptible to conflicts, which can only be resolved through effective communication.

We communicate when we pass a message from us to someone, for example, telling someone how you feel, or how you spent your day. Isn't that easy? Nevertheless, that may not be a productive conversation, or it's not where communication ends. We communicate effectively when we transfer our message clearly and appropriately to be understood or received by the listener. I have had instances where it seemed like I was talking to a rock, constantly repeating myself which is a clear indication that my message may not have been effectively communicated.

As *Pain Candidates,* sometimes, due to intense pain and frustration, we find it easier to pour out our emotions in an uncensored manner, believing that we've communicated. Yes, we might feel relieved after such an outburst, but the question is, would the listener have received the message? That is when we may make statements such as, "I feel like I have been talking to myself because nobody is listening!" You would be surprised that those around you are desperate to listen. And they are also willing to change, but the manner of communicating the message is becoming a barrier. Hence,

it is not what we say that matters, but how we say it. By statistics, our spoken words are 7%, our body language is 55%, and 38% is the tone of our voice. That implies, when we speak, the listener pays more attention to the message coming from our body language and the tone of our voice, than the actual spoken words.

In our journey from pain to gain, it is crucial to change our attitude towards our communication styles. Being able to manage our thoughts and emotions would significantly enhance our communication and relationships. We aim to create a conducive environment where we can communicate efficiently and be heard by those around us. Understanding to communicate is a skill and a topic which I would strongly encourage you to explore more, and one of the ways to learn and grow is through visualisation, which we shall discuss next. Visualisation becomes the hand that presents to you whatever you want to have and be. It became my companion and has always stuck with me through my journey from Pain to Gain.

It is vital to believe in yourself and your abilities, and it is necessary to respect and value your happiness.

CHAPTER 10

Step 8: Visualisation

If you can see what you want and how to get it,
you can have what you see.

What do you mentally see most of the time? Do you see Pain or Gain, success or failure?

Of course, we all visualise, but the only difference is that most of us, *Pain Candidates*, choose to see and receive only the wrong things. As discussed in Chapter Six:

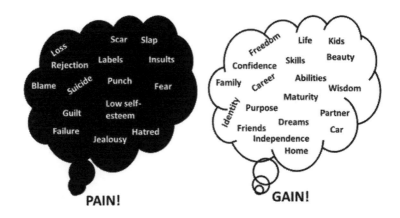

Our thought patterns condition us to be more prone to negative than positive thinking. Visualisation, mental descriptions, or mental rehearsal as it is referred to by many is a psychological technique that is used by many athletes to win in competitions. This 'secret to winning' technique, which became popular in sports around the 1960s, has benefited a lot of sporting champions. Before these athletes physically perform in any game, they would have, on many occasions, played mentally. That means, they would have allowed themselves to mentally go through the motion, to get a feel of what is going to happen in the physical. According to Dr Patrick J. Cohn (sport psychology expert),

"When athletes visualise or imagine a successful competition, they actually stimulate the same brain regions as you do when you physically perform that same action."

So, visualisation helps to condition the brain, boosting physical and emotional strength and optimism. In an online article by *The Guardian,*[7] Wayne Rooney, the England football striker, revealed that visualisation forms an integral part of his preparation. He said, "Part of my preparation is I go and ask the kit man what colour we're wearing – if it's red top, white shorts, white socks or black socks. Then I lie in bed the night before the game and visualise myself scoring goals or doing well. You're trying to put yourself in that moment

---

[7] https://www.theguardian.com/football/2012/may/17/wayne-rooney-visualisation-preparation

and trying to prepare yourself, to have a 'memory' before the game. I don't know if you'd call it visualising or dreaming, but I've always done it, my whole life...."

Although people attribute visualisation mostly to sports, it is a mental practice and a success secret that can be applied by anyone in any area of life - be it in health, career, finance, education, family, or relationships. By visualising, you could develop your skills, lose weight, have an ideal partner, get a perfect job, develop confidence, to name a few. I tested this to see if it works, and I was shocked by the physical reaction. What I did was to lie in bed, with my eyes closed and imagine myself jogging up my street. Within 5 - 10 minutes of visualising, I felt some sagittal movement, my heart started racing, and I began sweating. Not just that, I was highly motivated to jog physically.

Visualisation is also therapeutic when we focused on the positives. One afternoon, I was so overwhelmed with problems and decided to lay on the sofa with my eyes closed. About two minutes into my mental rehearsal, my son walked in and noticed I was smiling. He whispered to my daughter, saying, "Look at Mum; she's smiling in her sleep". Little did they know I was alert, but just daydreaming. Whenever I set my mind on my goals, I feel ecstatic, energetic, motivated and determined to keep working hard to achieve my dreams. Moreover, when I mentally live my dreams, I feel the joy of having them and my faith to obtain them grows stronger. Personally, visualisation has been one of my most significant influencing factors to achieving my goals. That is why I chose to include it as a crucial step in our journey to a thriving life.

Cultivating a habit of guided visualisation will enable us to turn our Pain into Gain.

Seeing is Believing

The first time I heard about visualisation was during my transformational journey. Reading through self-help books written by motivational speakers, athletic champions, entrepreneurs, and high-profile psychologists, I observed that they all touched on the concept of mental imagery. Out of curiosity, I delved deeper into unravelling what it was all about, and surprisingly, it was a core concept in my creator's manual (Bible). In fact, I would say it is the basis of my Christian faith. This is because it is written in the manual that, "**without faith,** it is impossible to please God...". And faith is defined in Hebrews 11:1 as,

> **"The substance of the things we hope for, the evidence of things not seen."**

No wonder, in numerous parts in the manual, we are told, "Fear not", "Have faith," "Everything is possible if you just believe". Now, let's put the religious aspect away and focus on the word faith. In any dictionary, faith is synonymous with confidence, optimism, hope, trust, positivity, belief and certainty. And what is life without these elements? For example, we go to bed at night with the confidence, or faith, that we'll wake the next morning. Or we drop our kids in school in the morning with certainty that we'll pick them after school. Or you invest in a project with faith that it will succeed. So, our daily life is lived by faith.

When I watched the movie, *The Secret*, directed by Rhonda Byrne, I was highly inspired by the success stories of some self-made millionaires and billionaires. It depicted how they used visualisation to attract the desires of their hearts. Many of them are living their dream lives, thanks to positive mental imagery. So, discovering the benefits, I started applying the technique to my everyday life. Whatever I hoped for, I saw it clearly in my mind. I visualised this book and believed that someday, you would be reading it, and it's now a reality. I envisioned myself delivering recovery and empowerment programs and speaking within my community, and they all became my reality. When we visualise and take necessary actions, we bring our dreams to reality. What is it that you would like to see come true in your life? You can take some steps today to achieve that dream.

**Visualisation triggers a similar response
from the autonomic nervous system, which
produces the same results as if in the physical.**

Join me - let's practise

I would encourage you to read these instructions and let's try visualisation to see the result. Put yourself in a relaxed position (either sitting upright or lying down) and reduce or eliminate any background noise. With your eyes shut, gently breathe in and out for about a minute to relax your muscles. Still keeping your eyes closed, bring to mind a picture of whatever you would like to see happen (it must be something positive). Ensure you put some details to your mental image - colour, taste, sound, smell, quantity and the like. Stay with the mental image for about five minutes and notice your body's reaction. How did you feel?

Each time I do this, it calms me down and leaves me feeling optimistic, happy, motivated, and loved. The best part for me is when I hold my images in greater details – pictures, sound, smell, feeling, surrounding, - and accompany these mental images with positive affirmations like:

- I am intelligent.
- I am loving, kind, patient, forgiving.
- I am going places and changing many lives.
- I am an incredible writer.
- I am an excellent motivational speaker.

When I affirm each statement, I also allow the mental image to flood my mind, focusing on it for about 1-2 minutes, then move to the next. Although it appeared time-wasting at first, I now find it one of the simplest things to do – it just comes to me naturally.

To thrive as Pain Candidates, we need to concentrate only on what we want – on honest, pure, lovely and beautiful thoughts. Hence, do your best to dispel the thoughts or images of the things that bring you hurt and stifle your growth. With the knowledge of mind control, I am confident that you can become the captain of your ship. This can also become easier when you choose to disrupt your comfort zone, which now takes us to the next step to turning your pain into gain. Remember, we said that our comfort zones are our most significant barriers to thriving. If we can disrupt this, we'll be halfway into accomplishing our dreams. For me, it was one of those areas which I struggled with until I devised a strategy that saved me.

> *"... whatsoever things are true, whatsoever things are honest, whatsoever things are just, whatsoever things are pure, whatsoever things are lovely, whatsoever things are of good report; if there be any virtue, and if there be any praise, think on these things."*

CHAPTER 11

Step 9: Interrupt Your Comfort Zone

"You never change your life until you step out of your comfort zone; change begins at the end of your comfort zone."
– Roy T. Bennett

Do you know that some people would rather die than to leave their comfort zones?

The term 'comfort zone' has become household jargon. And yes, we all have our physical and mental comfort zones – that space where we feel safe, comfy, and at ease with ourselves and others. Our comfort zones could be our home, relationship, job, academic position, social network, hobbies, financial status, health condition, thinking pattern, language, cultures, emotions, and behaviour. Although we might not be satisfied with our 'safe zones', yet we may choose to stay within them for varied reasons. For many *Pain Candidates* suffering from the brunt of limiting beliefs, our comfort zones may have been created from birth and reinforced through our childhood by those in our growth environment; and because we are rooted and grounded in our 'limiting safe zone' mindsets, altering it can become a nightmare.

For many years, I knew that I was struggling to cope in my relationship, but I chose to persevere because it was safer for me to try and fix things than to walk away. In the process, I became acquainted with the daily emotional discomfort, which gradually became my 'safe zone'. I didn't know what was outside the ordinary, so I accepted the experiences I was going through. Another comfort zone was my job. Even though I enjoyed my job, and my clients were happy, my talents were constrained. I was okay with just visiting my clients in their homes or residential homes and supporting them on a one-to-one basis, without having to stand in public and talk. Even when I finally found my purpose and I knew public speaking was part of it, I got numbed each time I thought of it. But guess what? Each time I brave it and speak, the result is always incredible!

Just like our unhealthy thought patterns, our comfort zones can also hold our lives HOSTAGE. This can affect our health, relationship with others, self-image, time, aspirations, personal and professional growth, and our energy. And when you hear people say, "get out of your comfort zone" it is not as simple as ABC. This is because if you have been accustomed to thinking, talking, and behaving in a certain way, it is not easy to suddenly change. Also, if you have been constantly labelled with negative tags like, "you're useless, ugly, foolish, a failure and incompetent", it may be challenging to swiftly block those voices from mentally echoing. As a result, we might find it easier to embrace these negative beliefs and opinions and, as such, it suffocates our growth.

One thing I was 100% convinced about, as the only way to achieving my dreams, was to step out of my safe zones. Given my ingrained limiting beliefs, I needed a step-by-step movement, which I called, '**The Zone-to-Zone**' method. This method required me to move in three stages:

1. The THINKING Stage
2. The EMOTION Stage
3. The BEHAVIOUR Stage

Each stage, beginning with the thinking stage, had five zones which I needed to stretch. These were zones 0, 1, 2, 3 and 4 as indicated in the diagram below. The thinking stage led to the emotion stage, and subsequently the behaviour stage. Likewise, a positive or negative reaction in one zone led to a corresponding result in the next zone. In the following sections, I will demonstrate how I walked through these stages to my present reality - thriving life.

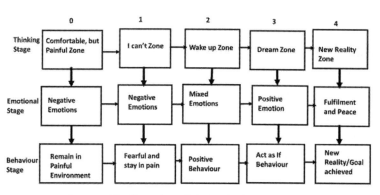

A summary of thoughts, emotions and behaviours based on my experience

In life, any change process begins with awareness. We need to ignite our consciousness to the fact that we have a comfort zone which needs stretching. This is the stage where we need to reflect on questions like, "What is my current comfort zone, and how is it restricting my growth and happiness? What is stopping me from stretching that comfort zone? What can I do differently to step out of that comfort zone? What are the benefits I will get If I stretch my comfort zone?" Pondering on these questions may be the start to stretching your comfort zones from zero to one, two, three and finally, zone four – where you create your new reality and live a thriving life.

Zone Zero - Thinking, Emotion and Behaviour Stages

Thinking - Zone zero (0) – This is the zone I called *a comfortable, but painful zone*. It was my usual limiting-thinking zone. It is the zone where I harboured all the negative voices, people's negative opinions, and my distorted thinking patterns. Within this zone, I felt comfortable with the distorted thought patterns. Each time, I focused on negative beliefs; I was emotionally drained. In this zone, my judgment was also clouded by the opinions of loved ones, which made it challenging to think rationally hence, leaving me with negative emotions.

Emotion - Zone zero (0) – This *comfortable, but painful zone* is the zone that creates all the negative emotions we can think of. As I focused on my limiting beliefs and negative opinions of others, I also created corresponding emotions like sadness, frustration, fear, shame, guilt, despair, and grief, which left me exhausted. As *Pain Candidates*, when we stay longer in this zone, we might end up developing mental illness that can be disabling. Thus, if this is how you feel, I urge you to step out of this zone as soon as you can and seek the necessary support.

Behaviour - Zone zero (0) – When we dwell on our limiting beliefs, the negative opinions of others and distorted thought patterns, we create negative emotions with corresponding behaviours. In my experience, I was disoriented and fearful, and the equivalent behaviour was to embrace the discomfort and stay within my painful environment.

Zone One - Thinking, Emotion and Behaviour Stages

Thinking - Zone one (1) - This is the zone I called, *I can't zone*. It is when I wasn't courageous enough to take any action, even though I knew I wasn't happy in my zone zero. It is also that zone where we give all the excuses why we cannot do or change something. We may make statements like, "I can't leave this environment; I can't speak up; I can't survive; I can't be confident; I can't live my dreams; I can't, I can't, I can't!" Although this zone is still a limiting mindset zone, at least it gives hope that something different can be done. It is usually just a matter of time to flip all the "I CAN'Ts" into "YES, I CAN!" And when we do, we move to zone two. However, when we don't, we stay in emotion zone 1.

Emotion - Zone one (1) – This *I can't* zone also creates negative emotions because we focus on our limitations. By using phrases like "I can't", "It is impossible", "It will never happen", it creates emotions like doubt, fear, frustration, anger, pessimism, anxiety, etc. To move to the next zone, we need to flip these statements. For me, I started convincing myself that, "Yes, I can leave this toxic environment. I can speak up. I can survive. I can be confident, and I can achieve my dreams". Just a simple act of flipping my negative phrases also changed my behaviour and stretched me from zone 1 to zone 2. But if I hadn't, I would have stayed in behaviour zone 1.

Behaviour - Zone one (1) – This *I can't* zone also aligns our behaviour to our thoughts and emotions. For instance, each time I said, "I can't leave, I can't speak up, I can't survive, I can't be confident, I can't live my dream", I felt doubtful, fearful, angry, unmotivated, and pessimistic. And my corresponding behaviour was to stay in my uncomfortable mental and physical environment. But when I started saying, "YES, I CAN!" I quickly moved into zone 2.

Zone Two - Thinking, Emotion and Behaviour Stages

Thinking - Zone two (2) - This is the zone I called *the wake-up zone*. It is when I was awoken to the fact that my zones zero and one were no longer comfortable, meaning I could no longer tolerate the emotional torture I was inflicting on me. It was also the stage where I had a genuine dialogue with myself, intending to root out my negativities. I realised that people's narrative of me was not my reality, and so, I needed to create a new reality for me. Besides, I needed to rewrite my story.

As *Pain Candidates,* this is the zone where we begin to challenge our negative beliefs and the negative views of others and find our uniqueness and purpose in life. For me, reading a self-help book, as mentioned at the start of this book, was my wake-up call. I hope that by sharing my journey, you will also wake up to that call of turning your pain into gain and stretching your zone.

Emotion - Zone two (2) – This *wake-up* zone may create mixed emotions. In my experience, when I finally woke up to the fact that I needed to create a new reality for me, I was excited, and, at the same time, nervous. It was that moment of self-education and discovering information that if I had known years back, my life or my relationship would have been more successful. And so, I felt angry and disappointed with myself for allowing my limiting mindset and people to hurt me. On the other hand, I felt relieved, hopeful, grateful, empowered, motivated and confident to rewrite my story. Maybe, by reading this book, you too could be feeling the same, but I can encourage you to look on the bright side. And I also urge you to wake up and act.

Behaviour - Zone two (2) – This *wake-up* zone creates positive thoughts and emotions that also awakens our positive behaviours. This is the zone where I engrossed myself in reading self-help books and attending recovery and empowerment programs. The success stories of other survivors inspired me. I created goals which I was determined to achieve, and the intensity of my positive emotions stretched me to zone 3.

Zone Three - Thinking, Emotion and Behaviour Stages

Thinking - Zone three (3) – This is the zone I called *the dream zone.* It is when I finally realised that I could achieve my dreams. This is also the zone where we begin to unlock our passions and potentials to reach our highest level of fulfilment. It is where we no longer focus on the negative past or people's negative opinions, but we 100% concentrate on us! This zone is all about you and your dreams in life.

When I was in this zone, I had written down clear targets to meet, ranging from career, financial, and relationship, to leisure, networking, and comfort. Interestingly, all the goals I had written were outwith my comfort zone. For example, my goal of becoming an author and a motivational speaker was frightening. Each time I read my mission statement and mentioned the term "public speaking", doubt and fear crept in. I couldn't achieve my goals without first stretching my comfort zones and secondly, overcoming my negative thinking patterns. I needed to convince my brain to recognise and accept the necessity for me stepping out of my comfort zone.

Each time I pondered on how life as an author, coach and motivational speaker would be, I felt empowered and excited, thus stretching my thinking zone.

Emotion - Zone three (3) – This *dream zone* is where positive emotions take over. Once we identify our uniqueness, set our goals, identify the benefits of our goals and know the steps to achieve them, we become invincible. In my case, each time I mused on my dream life, I felt more confident, optimistic, motivated, passionate, joyful, and the intensity of these feelings was energising. I was also ready to break every barrier and was fully persuaded to achieve my dreams. Think about this for a moment - If you were guaranteed to have whatever you want today, how would that make you feel?

-That's the kind of feeling I was experiencing in my dream world, and I loved it! I didn't want to let go, and this stretched me to take action!

Behaviour - Zone three (3) – This *dream zone* created unending positive thoughts and emotions, which translated into positive actions. This is the zone where I started talking and acting like an author, coach, motivational speaker, and, of course, like a CEO! At first, I was comfortably uncomfortable to be out of my comfort zone, but I was also determined to achieve my dreams, no matter what. So, my daily actions were stretching my comfort zone and creating a new reality for me. That is how I stretched to zone 4, and I am confident that you, too, can do the same.

Zone Four - Thinking, Emotion and Behaviour Stages

Thinking - Zone Four (4) – This is the zone I called **My New Reality zone.** It is the zone where, after going through all the other zones, I finally reached my new reality. I successfully replaced my distorted or irrational thinking patterns with positive ones. It is where we achieve our goals and rewrite our stories. Once again, just knowing that you're reading this book gives me the fulfilment of living my dream. The testimonies I receive give me joy that no amount of money can buy. Returning to Chapter Five, what's your purpose in life? Identifying and living your purpose will give you the same feeling of accomplishment.

Emotion - Zone four (4) – This *new reality zone* is my present zone. It is the zone where I felt fulfilled after all the hard work. As *Pain Candidates,* when we look back and see how far we have come, we feel accomplished and at peace with ourselves.

Behaviour - Zone four (4) – As already stated, this is the zone of our **new reality**. For you, it could be achieved in the next one month, six months, one year or even in the next ten years. For any *Pain Candidate* who may be thinking, "How can I leave this comfort zone?" My answer is that you might not leave the zone today or even in the next year. But if you're willing to interrupt that comfort zone by just one step, it will eventually lead you to your new reality.

> **In order for us to achieve something different, we must behave differently, and that involves stepping outside of our comfort zones.**

It is worthy of note that disrupting our comfort zone is a continuous cycle. You would notice that once you stretch one zone, it becomes a new comfort zone and to disrupt this new zone, you would need to go through the stages again. The good news is that, if you've done it once, you will find it easier to do it again. Your passion for thriving will break every barrier to living your dream life.

In our journey from pain to gain, we can't afford to stay in the same safe zone. Thankfully, you now have the technique of overcoming fear, and noting your progress, as seen in the next chapter, will facilitate your journey. Refuse to remain in that life-limiting zone. You have untapped potentials and ideas that can change the world. So, refuse to settle for less because you were born to **win and not to lose.**

CHAPTER 12

Step 10: Note -Record Progress

No matter how good or bad you think you are,
there is always room for improvement.

Which of the following statements do you identify with?

1. I feel that I am progressing in my life.
2. I feel that I am regressing in my life.
3. I feel stuck in my life.
4. None of the above.

Irrespective of which statement you choose, you must have a reason for it and that reason, most likely, will be based on the current results or happenings in your life -True or false? If I say, "I am thriving now", for example, that is because of the evaluated and recorded state of my wellbeing. We can't magically determine our level of growth without feedback or taking notes of the occurrences in our lives.

How do you know if you are a good parent, loving partner, dedicated and delightful colleague, good friend, or a good neighbour? It is through feedback! In the same manner, we may never know the worth and extent of our beliefs, capabilities, and accomplishments unless we get feedback from results and people. But how willing are we to welcome feedback?

Speaking with my *pain pals*, I noticed that many would usually not like to be told the truth about themselves. If someone has portrayed themselves as contrary to the reality, it becomes uncomfortable to accept the fact, especially from loved ones. Truth indeed hurts, but without it, we can't grow. No matter how good or bad you think you are, there is always room for improvement. And it is only through honest feedback that we can improve. Our poor behaviours, low performances, negative actions, or omissions may not be deliberate, yet if these are not producing positive results for us and those around us, this is worth addressing. Like any other behaviour, our attitude towards criticism might have been inherited or triggered by the contrary view or grudge we hold against the one giving it. This behaviour is typical amongst intimate relationships. I am sure you're familiar with those moments where we provide a valid reason for every poor behaviour, thus resisting the need to change. We also tend to accept feedback from a professional yet resist that same feedback from a loved one, just because it is coming from them. You can't say you know it all, neither can you minimise people for their feedback. Sometimes you can downplay or ignore it, but if you are wise, you will grasp the hidden truth and change your life.

Feedback may come from anyone (kids, family, friends, colleagues, strangers). It could also come from the results we get, such as medical reports, bank statements, kids' school reports, job promotion, level of confidence, etc. These are all clues that something is either right or wrong. No matter the source of your feedback, the most important thing is to take note of the result you are producing. As compliment-seeking creatures, we might not like to receive negative feedback, as well as the results we are creating, but the essential thing is to record the underlying message, address the situation and produce a better result. In other words, the Pain of negative feedback produces Gain for positive accomplishments. In the words of Colin Powell,

> **"Success is the result of perfection, hard work, learning from failures, loyalty, and persistence."**

A New Attitude to Feedback is Gainful

In our journey from pain to gain, changing our attitude towards feedback is vital for our personal development and happiness. As fallible beings, we need constant improvement. Thus, we're givers and receivers of feedback; and the results we get will depend on our attitudes. Sometimes, it is not the content of the feedback that is resisted, it is the attitude of the person giving it. Like any communication, it is not what we say that matters, but how we say it. In my view, if we love someone and want the best for them, we will give our feedback with love, respect, honesty, and empathy.

As receivers of feedback, the benefit lies in our attitude. We need to welcome and appreciate all feedback that comes our way and shouldn't be offended by people's nature of doing or saying things. Like Marc and Angel Chernoff said,

"You can't control how other people behave. You can't control everything that happens to you. What you can control is how you respond to all. In your response is your power."

During my *mental rebirth*, I cultivated a positive reaction to feedback and wanted to be accountable to myself, while also looking forward to welcoming others' views on my progress. I had a notebook which I titled, "my progress record" and I always left it by my bedside. I had written down all my improvement areas such as assertiveness, exercise, healthy diet, time management, study, quality time with kids, me time, listening, and so on. At the end of each day, I would score myself by asking questions like: On a scale of 1-10, how healthy did you eat today? How many new words did you learn today? How can you do better tomorrow?" Although I was sometimes hard on myself, it only motivated me to perform better. Just by reading one chapter each day, I read about one or two books each month. By learning a new word each day, I learned about 30 new words each month. Furthermore, by cutting down on time wasted on social media on unproductive content, I saved and dedicated my time to meaningful activities.

One of the bravest things I did was asking my kids to rate my parenting on a scale of 1-10. Although the first feedback was disappointing, I welcomed it! It was a wake-up call for me. Having to parent them to meet a certain standard, without feeling like I was failing, I certainly immersed myself in the daily parental routine without realising that I was losing touch with myself. My son said, "Mum, if you want to score 7-10, I suggest you do the following: Take off the "parent hat" of always trying to perfect things. Relax, laugh and joke more. Occasionally, ignore the dirty dishes, messy bedroom and late bedtime." At least, that feedback helped me to release my grip, and helped strengthened our relationship. Now, I'm always ready to ask and welcome feedback because it's a blessing.

It's a BLESSING

B – Be focus

L – Learn to appreciate

E - Evaluate

S - Strengthens

S – Strategize

I – Insight

N – No Guilt

G – Get on it

As a *Pain Candidate*, I approach all feedback with the attitude of, "**it's a BLESSING**". It is a blessing for me to learn and grow, triumph, turn my pain into gain and live a thriving life. I usually don't bother whether the feedback-giver despises me or loves me; or whether the feedback is balanced or biased. Again, we cannot control people's opinion or beliefs about us, but we can control the way we want to respond. One thing I always tell myself is that *"this advice has something to benefit me. I will extract the good and bin the rest"*. And so, if it is a blessing for us, we should also receive it with BLESSING.

Be Focus –Before my *mental rebirth*, whenever someone was giving me feedback, especially a negative one, I would be quick to defend myself. As a result, I would usually miss half of the message. Now I understand that to benefit from feedback, I need to pay attention to what is being communicated. Being focus means active listening and making the messenger feel appreciated – after all, it's your blessing!

Learn to Appreciate – It is also a kind gesture to thank people for their feedback, even when their feedback is negative, or their delivery style is hostile. They may also be expressing their frustration, so be objective and empathetic. No amount of defence or blaming will help. Remember, **we take what is useful for our development and ditch the rest.**

Evaluate – Evaluation begins with genuineness. We need to be honest about ourselves and our performance. Evaluate the areas you are not great at, and ask questions like, "What is causing it?" "Based on the feedback, how could I be better?" Remember, this whole process is about your growth, not someone else. It is your blessing. And during that evaluation, you will also be surprised that you've had plenty more successes than failures.

Strengthens/ Support – Once you evaluate the situation and understand the cause of any poor performance, you will need to improve yourself by reaching out to those that can support you to perform better. We may also read books, articles, and other resources on the subject. During those challenging moments, endeavour to spend time with positive people who understand your value and can boost your confidence.

Strategize – Once we know the area of improvement, how to improve it, and the support network, it is time to strategize. You will need to create a road map that will help you arrive at the desired change destination. To know whether we are reaching our goals, we need to set performance indicators. For me, my performance indicator for becoming an author was ensuring to write at least two paragraphs each day. So long as I was complying with my daily target, I was confident of reaching my destination – This Book.

Insight – It may be helpful to get some ideas or opinions about your strategy. You could speak to a boss, colleague, friend, or mentor, to get their insight on your road map. They might add some valuable suggestions that could make things easier for you. Remember, it is all about seeking the support you need.

No Guilt – Do not waste your time blaming others. There is no need to feel guilty or bad for not performing well. Even as you work on improving, things can still go wrong. Do not have any sense of guilt. It's a lesson and a blessing – embrace it!

Get on! – Just get on with the job. Do what you need to do and when you do, you'll be glad you did. Your feedback will become your blessing. With some goal-setting skills, as discussed in the next chapter, you will turn negative feedback to your gain. Our lives begin and end with setting goals, that is why it is key to turning our pain into gain.

We may never know the worth and extent of our beliefs, capabilities and accomplishments unless we get feedback from results and people.

CHAPTER 13

Step 11 – Goal-Setting

*"Setting goals is the first step in turning the
invisible into the visible."*
– Tony Robbins

The first time I delivered the TYPIG[8] training, a *Pain Candidate* asked: "Why did you leave the goal-setting to this point? I would have thought it would be the first on the list…" Just before I could answer, she interrupted and said, "Oh, I know! It is because without achieving the first ten steps, it would be difficult to achieve our goals…" "Perfect answer!" I responded.

What is goal-setting? It is all about deciding what you want to achieve and creating a clear plan on how to achieve it. How many times have you set a goal and didn't achieve it because you were psychologically unstable? If you noticed, all the above chapters are focused on our psychological wellbeing. Each one has been equipping us with tools and techniques

---

[8] Turning Your Pain into Gain

to take charge of our minds and ourselves. We've learned not to allow people and events to dictate how we want to live our lives. Although achieving the first ten steps also requires goal-setting, it was more about developing our inner qualities to facilitate our success in whatever goal we set. Hopefully, you are now excited about your aspirations and can utilize your unique strengths to turn your pain into gain.

No Goals, No Life

Right now, you have a goal you would like to achieve – true or false? And If you ask anyone around you, including kids as young as two years old, they will say the same – they always want something.

We are a goal-setting species. We love setting goals and desiring to achieve goals. Right now, you may be wishing to go on holiday, be promoted at work or get into a new career. Or, you might be longing to have an intimate partner, have kids, make money, have a comfy car, buy a house, end that abusive relationship, open that business and many others - No goals, no life. When we don't set goals, we live life with no focus and direction, and life itself may have no meaning. Like a road map, goal-setting tells us whether we are on track or off track, succeeding or failing, and it gives us a sense of achievement and self-actualisation. The reason why we live and wish to see the next day is because of our aspirations! But like we said, our abilities to achieve our varied goals may be thwarted by our lack of emotional stability.

For many years, I was setting goals which I hardly accomplished. I used to start projects and healthy habits but abandoned them unexpectedly due to varied reasons. Goal-setting didn't seem a valuable exercise because mine were never achieved due to a lack of inner drive. And as we're aware, it is easier to blame it on something or someone when our goals are not achieved, rather than addressing ourselves and our emotions. During my growth journey, it dawned on me that I needed to first work on myself before attempting to set any goal. It was also necessary to be intentional about my goals and not let myself be distracted by people or events. Furthermore, going at my pace was vital, but also taking into consideration the impact of my goal on others. Personally, the determining factor for successfully achieving my goals has been a positive mindset and emotional stability.

Where Are You Heading To?

In one of my training sessions, I asked one of the *Pain Candidates,* "Can you tell me where you would like to be in five years?" And she laughed and said, "I don't know, I might be dead by then - who knows?!" Well, I must admit that death is inevitable, and the thought alone is the more reason why you need to set goals that facilitate your life's direction. We shouldn't live life based on luck or coincidence; we need to be deliberate on what we want. It isn't just about saying, "I want a good job" or "I want plenty of money" or "I want good health." Goal-setting requires careful reflection and consideration of what you want, how you want it, and when you want it. It also requires determination, hard work and consistency. And the BIG one – it needs to be written down! Don't just have it in your mind; **write it down**.

Our goals can be immediate or short-term (0 – 1year), medium (1-3 years) and long-term (3-5 years and above). Goals can also be set on a daily, weekly, monthly, and yearly basis. My daily goals = my weekly goals = my monthly goals = my yearly goals. It is always comforting to know that every action I take amounts to the bigger success.

During my *mental rebirth* journey, I realised that the first thing I needed to do was to learn how to set Specific, Measurable, Attainable, Relevant, and Timed (SMART)[9] goals, which has been crucial in turning my pain into gain. The second thing was to set goals that were meaningful to me and something I was passionate about. The third thing was to prioritise my goals. These are key factors which I never used to consider; no wonder I was starting and abandoning projects halfway through because I either didn't like it, was overburdened or lacked the resources.

Grab a Pen and a note pad - let's do this

Specific Goal: Now, pause for a moment – you may close your eyes and take a deep breath. Bring to mind what you want to achieve, preferably a short-term goal. Try to answer these questions: What specifically do I want? Why do I want it? What do I need to achieve it? Who will be involved?

Measurable goal: Now, let's ensure we track your success and keep you motivated. Answer these questions: How would I know that I have achieved my goal? How much or how many of it do I want? For example, if you said you wanted to

---

[9] https://www.mindtools.com/pages/article/smart-goals.htm

build your self-confidence; what does self-confidence mean to you? How would you know that you are self-confident?

Attainable goals: Next, let's ensure your goal is reasonable and attainable. We also want to stretch your comfort zone, but ensuring that you do not get overwhelmed. So, answer these questions: How can I accomplish this goal? Do I have the time, money, energy, or resources? Would I need to stretch myself or my resources? Would it affect anyone? What will stop me from achieving it? How can I overcome any barrier?

Relevant goals: We need to ensure that your goal is crucial to you and fits with other important goals in your life. So, we don't want other goals to disrupt this specific goal. Answer yes or no – Is this the right thing to do? Is this the right time to do it? Am I the right person to do it? Will it improve other areas or things in my life?

Set time: We need to ensure that you have a specific date and something to look forward to. By having a deadline, you can be motivated to prioritise your everyday tasks to achieving your goal. So, answer these questions: When do I want to achieve my goal? (date - day/month/year). What can I do six months from now? What can I do six weeks from now? What can I do today? **Well done!**

Now that you have your SMART goal(s) written down, you are good to go! Do not delay it – start today. I also encourage you to put your SMART goal into a statement of purpose - a written statement which outlines your specific goals as if already achieved. When I set my goals of being an author, wellbeing trainer and motivational speaker, I wrote a statement as follows:

> *"It is 30th September 2021. I have published one self-help book, spoken at 20 events, delivered 50 recovery workshops, changed 5000 lives, and I am overjoyed and feeling very blessed."*

My statement of purpose has been my most excellent motivator. I have a copy on my vision board, located by my bedside, and another in my purse, which I read at least once a day. Each time I feel distracted or am procrastinating, I hold myself accountable for the content of my statement.

I must applaud you to have diligently gone through our TYPIG journey from step one to step 11. Now that you have successfully laid the foundation for turning your pain into gain, and having your specific goal(s), the remaining three steps are the bonus steps, and are vital to transforming your dreams into reality. It is to give you the mindset of a real go-getter – a "No Matter What" mentality.

The reason why we live and wish to see the next day is because of our aspirations!

CHAPTER 14

Step 12 - No Matter What

"Life is a battle; those who give up become losers. Be prepared to fight until you win."
– Susan Changsen

Imagine yourself, trapped in a jungle, and you need only one thing to survive and rescue yourself. What would it be?

Whenever I ask this question, I hear responses like food, water, a map, safety, and of course, willpower, which is my preferred answer.

'No Matter What' is a statement of determination, faith, courage, and resilience. It takes away all barriers to achieving our goals and forces us to take risks, overcome challenges and refuse to accept the obvious. It also tells us to see the light at the end of the tunnel. When we cultivate the 'No Matter What' mindset, we become invincible to trials in life. That means, we conquer our fears, take back control of our lives, find our voices, command power, find our purpose, turn our Pain into Gain and live a thriving life.

I watched with awe the fighting spirit of my granny. She was a woman with a 'No Matter What' mentality. She never believed in losing battles; even when she didn't succeed, she came out stronger. I listened to her one night as we talked while enjoying some roasted maize and freshly boiled peanuts, which is one of those unforgettable memories. Although we were poor monetarily, we were rich in inner peace of mind and bounty of nature. During harvesting season, after the day's hard labour, Granny and I would sit around the fireplace as she educated me with words of wisdom.

I already knew that she had 13 children and lost nine of them. However, what I wasn't aware of, and which I never bothered to ask, was the reason for their deaths and the circumstances in which they died. So, this night happened to be the night that Granny opened up to tell me how each child died and what she endured. After experiencing five still-births and losing four grown-up kids, she became a widow with four surviving kids to take care of. She was not only going through the never-ending grief, but also enduring the pressure of obnoxious traditional practices. She resisted the customary demands to marry her brother-in-law. As a result, and to intimidate her into surrendering, they confiscated all valuable possessions, rendering Granny and the kids homeless.

It was heart-breaking listening to her as she narrated her agony with a smile on her face, which made me sick to my stomach. I lost my appetite that night and couldn't stop sobbing, but as I did, she never stopped talking. In hindsight, maybe she too was releasing what she had bottled up for years, and she felt good about it. At every interval, she tapped me on the shoulder and gave me this look as if to say, "This stuff is for your good".

I can also recall that at one moment during that conversation, I became so furious, not just at the in-laws, but at Granny. I interrupted her, as she narrated the ordeal, and I angrily looked straight into her eyes and I said, "But Grandma, why didn't you just accept the tradition and save your children and yourself from pain?" She paused - took a deep breath and with a captivating smile, she continued narrating the tormenting experiences. When she finished, she turned to me, held my hands, and said,

> *"My child, if you live your life on this earth, wanting to please people or lose your identity to live life for others, then you have wasted the purpose for which you were born... that is why I refused to let them rule me..."*

Back then, I didn't grasp the meaning of her statement, but now I understand what it means to lose your identity because of fear. She had refused to become their slave and like a voiceless lamb led to the slaughter. In the end, when these in-laws realised that she was a hard nut to crack, they gave up. And guess what? My granny died with her dignity intact, leaving an incredible legacy for her generation. Today, she still has her four surviving children, 15 grandchildren and 19 great-grandchildren and counting. That is the price of having a "No matter what" mentality.

You might have read the above paragraphs, and they ignited memories of similar experiences, either as a child or an adult. Thankfully, you survived it, or your family survived it. What you need now is the willpower to keep going. Having a 'No Matter What' attitude makes you a champion (so to speak). It helps you to hold your head above water, knowing full well that you'll survive. When you know who you are, you will refuse to let circumstances and people dictate your life. When you also know what you want in life, you will endure all odds to navigate your way to success. With this mindset, when circumstances present the contrary, you'll stand tall and tell yourself that, NO MATTER WHAT:

- I will resist!
- I will take back control of my life!
- I will become who I was born to be!
- I will learn to be confident!
- I will face my fears!
- I will gain that qualification!
- I will get that job!
- I will go back to school!
- I will come out of my comfort zone!
- I will develop healthy habits and thinking patterns!
- I will read that book!
- I will burn those calories and be healthy again!
- I will start that business!

These positive affirmations encourage and motivate you to keep resisting the temptation to quit. It zones out the negative voices that try to discourage you. It also makes you want to keep fighting for what is right and just. However, this willpower is a daily endeavour, and it begins immediately you wake up in the morning – with gratitude and enthusiasm. Ask yourself each morning – "What are my objectives for today?" Whatever it is, I will achieve it, No Matter What!

As we mentioned earlier, any effort made towards your end goal is never small. Your daily goals = weekly goals = monthly goals = yearly goals = your dream. Some days, we may set goals and not achieve them due to one thing or the other; that is fine so long as we get back on track as soon as possible; we shall still achieve our end goals. Our daily mantra should be, **"I will turn my Pain into Gain, No matter What!"** "**I will live a thriving life, No Matter What!**" Our optimism, as discussed in the next chapter, should never cease. We should stop at nothing until we live the life that we so desired – Hard work, determination and positivity do pay off. As Hope Hicks puts it,

"There is no substitute for hard work. Never give up. Never stop believing. Never stop fighting."

CHAPTER 15

Step 13 – Optimism

"A Pessimist sees the difficulty in every opportunity;
an optimist sees the opportunity in every difficulty."
– Winston Churchill

We had just finished attending a Christmas play at my son's school, and as we walked out of the hall, he looked at me and said, "Mum, do you know if I had wings like those angels, I could fly?" "Really?" I responded with amazement. Quickly and energetically, he said, "Yes! I can fly! I can fly like a bird and like Superman. I can fly to Mexico ..." He was just four years old, and for some reason, he loved Mexico. That happened to be the only name he grasped from the map of North America, which was displayed in his classroom. He was very convinced and optimistic that if provided with wings, he could fly. How could I have told him that he couldn't? I would have dashed his hopes and made him to look stupid. Kids believe they can do everything if given the opportunity, until we interrupt with the "No, you can't".

In retrospect, the experience communicated a massive lesson to me. If only *Pain Candidates* had that mindset of impossibility, we could fly! Not literally, but metaphorically in every area of our lives. Flying could mean soaring emotionally, physically, financially, academically, spiritually, socially, and romantically. Besides, we will know that whatever we set our hearts and minds on, and with the right actions taken, we would achieve it. For my son, he needed some physical wings to fly. For me, I needed some 'mental wings' to fly - reasons why I embarked on a *mental rebirth*. I needed to rewire my brain, ridding it of limiting beliefs and becoming more optimistic. Once I did that, I started **seeing opportunities in every difficulty**. What can you see in that difficulty you're currently facing?

Personally, optimism is what makes us go to bed, knowing that we will wake up the next morning. Although we may not understand what happens around us as we sleep, we're hopeful that we will see the next day. Optimism is HOPE, and life ceases to exist from the moment we lose hope. Furthermore, optimism gives you the comfort and assurance that you'll succeed in turning your pain into gain, no matter what. It is an unwavering faith to change your present circumstances.

Optimism is not about being "delusional or madly over-confident." Moreover, optimism doesn't mean negating circumstances beyond our control and hoping we can change them overnight. Like the weather, we can't stop the rain from falling, but we can get an umbrella and function under the downpour. So too, we can't alter certain occurrences, but we can choose an attitude that will keep us living our lives happily.

Pessimism, on its part, is not a destroyer, as some may perceive. However, it becomes destructive when it gets to the extreme. Pessimism, in a reasonable proportion, creates optimistic options or possibilities for overcoming hopelessness. For instance, If I am reasonably pessimistic that I may not pass an exam, that will persuade me to intensify my study and preparedness for the exam, hence boosting my confidence of passing the exam.

Her Optimism Healed Her Affliction

Permit me to share with you a story that has always stuck with me. If there is one story that gave me hope from the Creator's manual, it is the story of the woman with the issue of blood (Mark 5:24).

This woman had suffered from a haemorrhage for 12 years. She had sold all her possessions and suffered a great deal under the care of many doctors, and had spent all she had, yet instead of getting better, she grew worse. This lady was also rejected by her community because of the stench that was oozing from her. The pain of her illness physically and emotionally tortured her, and all her hopes of being healed had dissipated.

One day, this woman heard that Jesus was passing through her town. She had heard of the many miracles that he had performed. She understood how busy Jesus was and the possibility that she may never meet him face-to-face. But she was also determined that she would not let that opportunity pass by - she was going to get her healing, no matter what. This woman thought to herself, *"If only I could touch the hem of Jesus' garment, I will be healed"*. And so, she waited, and when the day came, she activated her thoughts into action. I can imagine she had completely forgotten the fact that she was smelling. Moreover, she ignored the voices of those who mocked her, and she took the bold step to achieve her dream (healing).

Because of the crowd, it was difficult to get closer to Jesus, but she pressed forward. I can also imagine people trying to push her off the crowd because of her condition, but she remained adamant. Her mind was fixed on her thought - *"If only I could touch the hem of His garment, I will be healed"*. That optimism of receiving her healing motivated her the more to force herself towards Jesus. She finally squeezed through and touched the hem of Jesus' garment, and immediately her bleeding stopped. Noticing that power had left him, Jesus turned and asked, "Who touched my clothes?" And his disciples said, "You see the people crowding against you, and yet you ask, 'Who touched me?'" But Jesus kept looking round to see who had touched him. Then this woman, knowing what had happened to her, stepped forward, fell at the feet of Jesus, trembling with fear and narrated her agony. Jesus said to her, "Daughter, your faith has healed you. Go in peace and be freed from your suffering." Wow! What a story! What an optimistic woman!

As a *Pain Candidate,* when I read this story, I learned a few lessons. Firstly, this lady had suffered untold pain and had exhausted all her options to be healed. That pain for you may be ill health, emotional or physical abuse, mental health, bereavement, financial hardship, challenging kids, difficult boss, demanding job, etc. For some, they might have given up on life; for others, they may not have tried because of fear, limiting beliefs, societal pressure, people's opinions, just to name a few. We all, in one way or the other, fit into the shoes of this woman. We all have pain.

Optimism is often expressed at the point of expectation and desperation. When we are faced with challenges and seeking a solution, we have no choice other than to be hopeful. This is when others may have the 'child-like' faith of, "nothing is impossible". Others may say, "Although not everything is possible, I will do what it takes to achieve what is possible for me – my needs shall be met at the point of my faith". Most importantly, while others could be expecting a massive leap, you and I can focus on tiny and steady steps towards our dreams. In this journey of life, others may be running at 90 miles, 70 miles, 40 miles and even 30 miles per hour, but at the end of the day, if each one maintains their respective lanes and speed, we will all get to our destinations. The determining factor is whether you are willing to get to your destination. If you are, nothing should stop you.

The second lesson learned from the story is that this lady knew that Jesus was passing through her town, which tells me that she was alert to what was happening in her community. How many of us are aware of the innumerable growth opportunities within our communities? You would be surprised that just by asking, you could obtain the solution to that problem which is causing you sleepless nights.

Again, although this lady had exhausted all her options, that didn't mean she couldn't get her healing. She changed her mindset and expanded her possibilities for healing. At first, she focused only on medical treatment, but this time, she concentrated on her faith.

Similarly, when I left my relationship, I thought that was the end of my life because I had been made to believe that I was a failure and wouldn't achieve anything good in life. But when I refused to allow my past and the present circumstances to define my future, I started seeing possibilities. I chose to give myself another chance, and like this lady, I challenged and ignored those limiting voices. I told myself, *"If only I could turn my pain into gain, I would become a fulfilled woman."* And I did! Have you given up in life? Have you shut your eyes and ears to opportunities that can transform your life? Are you still listening to those that are trying to stop you from getting your healing?

Thirdly, this lady set a SMART goal. Her goal to get healed was specific, measurable, achievable, realistic and time-bound. It was specific in that she knew precisely what she wanted - her healing. It was measurable, in that her faith was great enough to get her full healing. The testimonies of others aroused her level of faith. She was confident that if she only touched the hem of Jesus' garment, she would get her healing. This lady was also realistic of the effort she needed to put in to achieve her healing. Forcing herself through the crowd wasn't easy, but she did it. And lastly, she was time conscious not to miss Jesus, and she knew that her healing would occur immediately she touched the hem of Jesus' garment. In the same way as I read other's books and was motivated by their stories, I hope that this book also gives you hope - as a *Pain Candidate*, you too can get healed. You too can bounce back to life.

The last thing I admire is her boldness to action, which we'll talk about in the next chapter. The only way she needed to turn her dream into reality was to **Get Up** and join the crowd. I am sure it was a crowd of *Pain Candidates* like herself. Sitting at home, or in the same position of pain, wouldn't have given her healing. In as much as people may sympathise with you, they can't change your circumstances. They may provide a temporary solution, but what you need is a permanent solution, and only you can get it. Only you can step out and change your life. And I hope you do it today.

CHAPTER **16**

Work Now - Take Consistent Action

*"The universe doesn't give you what you ask for
with your thoughts – it gives you what you demand
with your actions."*
- Steve M.

This is that moment where you could be saying, "Ok, Peggy, I've read that I need to ignite consciousness, accept responsibility, recondition my mind, set healthy habits, let go... and then what?" Fantastic! Now the only thing you need to do is to TAKE ACTION. If life was all about reading, talking and wishing, wouldn't it be great? Just imagine you talking and wishing about something, then, **BOOM!** It appears. Wouldn't that be perfect?

I remember reading a primary school storybook, about a poor orphan who fell in love with a Prince. Every night before she slept, she said a prayer in her heart and wished for an item. When she woke up each morning, she found her wishes, delivered by the Prince. This routine continued until she stopped asking, with the assumption that the Prince already knew her needs. However, immediately she stopped asking, the Prince also stopped giving. She became furious and demanded answers to why she couldn't get her wishes anymore. And the simple response from the Prince was, "because you stopped asking." Indeed, the universe is always ready to deliver our desires, but we need to play our part to make it come true. This is where taking action comes into place.

We have been 'talking' from the introduction, right up to this point. I have shared my experiences and those of others. We have shared tools and techniques which we can use to turn our pain into gain, and all this valuable information will be useless if we do not put them into action. Like I mentioned, until we realise that "talk is cheap, and action is gain", we will not change from the current position. For some people, that would mean finish reading this book and not applying the principles to change their lives. And I hope that is not you. We need to get to the point where we begin to start putting these ideas, our decisions, and goals into action.

Before now, I spent nearly all my time talking, complaining and planning about the positive change I wanted to see in my life. But I never dared to take the necessary actions needed to activate the change. Either I was scared to act or I wasn't prepared enough to work. Fear was always keeping me hostage. Even before I finally decided to publish this book, I was still overpowered with the thought of, "It still needs to be perfected." As a result, I kept editing the text and procrastinating on the publishing date. But I got to the point where I said, "You know what? I am just going to publish whatever I have written." I needed to move from deciding to doing. Sometimes, it pays to take the leap of faith and watch things unfold in your favour. What I do know is that, once we have a clear idea of our desires, and have evaluated the necessary risk, and put in place essential steps to minimise it, all we need is to act. Even if we make mistakes along the process, it becomes a learning curve for our development.

The Preparation and Waiting is Enough

I have spoken to my *pain pals* who have been planning and organising to do things for years. Some have had to apply for a provisional driving licence twice, because each time they got one, they delayed their driving test until the provisional licence expired. While others have been planning to register for college courses for years, some have been complaining of their abusive relationships or nagging boss for years. It can sometimes be frustrating to keep talking about the same thing for years. If what is holding you back is beyond your control (like health), it is understandable. But if it is because the time is not right, I am sorry to disappoint you that the time will never be right. The planning will never be perfect; the skills will never be enough; the fear will never go away; people will never stop talking; people will never stop judging you; the circumstances may never change until you decide to do something about it. Unfortunately, NOBODY can rescue you except YOURSELF. Sadly, there will never be another perfect time to act than NOW. The best way to get results is to stop talking, get up and do it. That is the only way you can show how intentional you are about turning your pain into gain. And so, I implore you to:

1. Wake up! Ignite consciousness to the present condition. Tell yourself that "enough is enough". Overcome the fear of taking necessary actions.
2. Take responsibility for your life.
3. Find your life purpose or what will give you meaning.
4. Start working on your thinking pattern.
5. Create new healthy habits.
6. Let go! Forgive yourself and those that have offended you, knowing that the exercise is for your benefit.
7. Sort out your relationships. Who is most important to you? Those that are least important and holding you back, let them go.
8. Start visualisation – mentally see the things you want to achieve in your life.
9. Leave your comfort zone and anything that has been holding you hostage.
10. Start paying attention to the feedback you are getting from your actions and omissions. This feedback will communicate valuable information to transform your life.
11. Unleash your power of goal-setting, which will facilitate the actions you take.
12. Cultivate the "No Matter What" attitude.
13. Be optimistic about the options you have in life. Believe that you have what it takes to rescue you.

All these require consistent action to bring them to fruition. Once you begin to take daily steps that align with these areas, you will start to see results. You will also notice that you are attracting all the necessary support you need, resources, people, finance, ideas, strengths, courage and the list goes on. Things will start to become more evident to you than you ever imagined. I am confident that there is no secret to turning your pain into gain; simply act on these 14 steps. There is also no secret to success other than taking bitesize actions. Like Mark Twain rightly states,

> *"The secret of getting ahead is getting started. The secret of getting started is breaking your complex overwhelming tasks into small manageable tasks, and then starting on the first one."*

No Action, No Gain

I have always been inspired by the Pain to Gain stories of some top celebrities. You would think that they painlessly walked themselves to the top of their careers, but that's not true. Many of them were once in the same position as you and me. They encountered dreadful conditions, yet they chose to work and turned their pain into gain. Permit me to share a few of these Pain to Gain Heroes with you.

In an online article by Huffington Post[10], titled, **"8 Celebrities Who Transformed Tragedy into Something Positive"**, some celebrities shared how they transformed their pain into gain. Among them are the following:

The first: Oprah Winfrey, whom I can describe as a champion for the education of females; proprietor of female

---

[10] https://www.huffingtonpost.co.uk/entry/celebrities-overcoming-loss_n_5669363

educational institutions; proprietor of the Oprah Winfrey Network as well as other programs, was sexually and physically abused. She is said to have been sexually abused by several family members at the age of 10. At 14, she became pregnant, but unfortunately, lost her baby boy after birth. Oprah is said to have kept these tragedies secret until a relative shared her story in the press in 1990, which became a relief. Despite her trauma, she was determined to get educated, and she graduated with honours from high school. She was then awarded a full college scholarship to pursue her education. Today, she has not just transformed her life, but the lives of millions across the globe. She couldn't have got where she is today if she didn't take some bold steps or actions to turn her Pain into Gain. Is that childhood shame and trauma still holding you back? I encourage you to do something different today to turn that Pain into Gain.

The second: Joaquin Phoenix, whom I can also describe as one of the most admired American actors, lost his brother to a drug overdose. Although he made the 911 call in an attempt to save his brother, unfortunately, his brother didn't make it. Phoenix was much traumatized, especially with the flow of negative media following the incident. This made him take a backstep in his career. Besides, he suffered addiction problems, and he sought professional help for alcoholism in 2005. Despite all of these, he managed to turn his life around. Twenty years later, he is now thriving in his career as an actor. Not only that, but he is also a social activist for organizations like Amnesty International, the Art of Elysium, HEART and Peace Alliance. Without taking actions, he wouldn't have turned his Pain into Gain. Are you allowing guilt or addiction to suppress your dreams? You too can choose to take action today, seek professional help and turn your Pain to Gain.

The third: Charlize Theron, whom I can describe as one of the most confident and brightest South African actresses, at the age of 15, witnessed her mother shoot and kill her alcoholic and abusive father out of self-defence. Despite the trauma, she did not allow her Pain to define her future. Using her mother's protective example of strength, she worked hard to build a high level of confidence in herself, which ultimately, boosted her career as an actress, making her the first South African actress to win an Academy Award. Charlize chose to act in changing her life. She used the lessons learned as an anchor to turn her Pain into Gain. What lessons have you learned from that Pain? How can you use it to change your life and those around you?

I can continue to cite thousands more examples, but these three are representative of how *Pain Candidates* can transform their Pain into Gain.

My dear *Pain Candidate*, I am sharing these stories to let you know that it takes just a single thought, decision and step to turn that Pain into Gain. These are evidence that the stigma of our emotional and physical pains can be transformed into strength, and this strength becomes our anchor to thrive in life. Now that I have given you the tools to transform your life, it is my wish that you, the reader, will use the strength gained in your Pain to your advantage. It is also my wish to see you move from point P (pain), where you are now, to point G (gain), where you want to be. It is my wish that you will take the 14 outlined steps, from Igniting consciousness to taking action, and if you do all these, I am highly confident that you will Turn Your Pain into Gain and live a THRIVING life. What are you waiting for? Take that first Step Now and make your Dream a Reality.

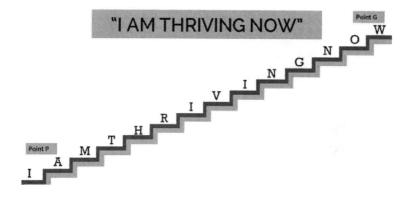

Please Stay in Touch

I would love it that we stay in touch. As a next step for you, I have carefully prepared a fantastic beginner self-growth package for you – THE 5 STEPS TO KICK START YOUR JOURNEY FROM TRAUMA TO TRIUMPH. The first session is free, and you get the following benefits:

- Reduce anxiety and despair
- Enhance the clarity of your life and a way forward.
- Gain Confidence and Peace of mind
- Save your time, money, and energy
- Increase your motivation to rekindle your sparkle
  Plus, you get the chance to work with me on a 1-2-1 and feature on my Magazine, whenever you are ready. Just click www.iamthrivingnow.com for more information. I have created the website and made it a welcoming and comfortable home for you, because you are incredibly special!

To get more inspirational messages that can help you through your Pain to Gain journey. I invite you to follow me on Facebook, Instagram, Twitter and LinkedIn with the handle @Peggy Bareh. You can also visit my sociatap link to access all my social media pages.

https://sociatap.com/PeggyBareh

I would really love to hear from you. Tell me how this book has helped you. Let me get your feedback. You can email me at Iamthrivingnow20@gmail.com or peggy@iamthrivingnow. com Be the first to know about the next book to be published.

References

Seligman, M.E.P et Al. (1990) "Explanatory Style as Mechanism of Disappointing Athletic Performance. "Psychological Science 1.p 143 -46.

Martin E.P. Seligman (2011) Flourish: A New Understanding of Happiness and Well-being – and How to Achieve Them. Nichola Brealey Publishing

A. H. Maslow (1943) A Theory of Human Motivation. Wilder Publications, Inc.

James Borg (2014) Mind Power: Change your thinking, change your life. Pearson Education Limited

Beck, A.T(1976). Cognitive therapies and emotional disorders. New York: New American Library

Daniel G. (1996) Emotional Intelligence: Why IT CAN MATTER MORE THAN IQ. Bloomsbury Publishing.

Burns, D.D. (2012) Feeling good: The mood therapy. New American Library

https://www.sciencefocus.com/the-human-body/why-do-newborn-babies-cry/

https://www.iasp-pain.org/Education/Content.aspx?Item
Number=1698

Luciani, J. (2015). Why 80 Percent of New Year's Resolutions
Fail. Retrieved from https://health.usnews.com/health-news/
blogs/eat-run/articles/2015-12-29/why-80-percent-of-new-
years-resolutions-fail

https://www.peaksports.com/sports-psychology-blog/
sports-visualization-athletes/

https://www.simplypsychology.org/maslow.html

https://www.psychologytoday.com/gb/blog/the-new-resilience/
201310/why-the-impact-child-abuse-extends-well-adulthood

https://www.pnas.org/content/early/2013/09/18/1315458110
**Childhood abuse, parental warmth, and adult multisystem
biological risk in the Coronary Artery Risk Development
in Young Adults study**

https://www.theguardian.com/football/2012/may/17/wayne-
rooney-visualisation-preparation

Suggested Books to Read

These are just a few books that helped to change my life, you may be interested to begin with. There are many others you can search. Start feeding your mind with new food.

1. The power of the Subconscious Mind (Dr. Joseph Murphy)
2. Mind Power: Change your thinking, change your life (James Borg)
3. Brilliant Positive Thinking (Sue Hadfield)
4. How to Get from Where You Are to Where You Want to Be (Jack Canfield)
5. Think and Grow Rich (Napoleon Hill)
6. Self-Reliance (Ralph Waldo Emerson)
7. Universal Laws (Creed McGregor)
8. Emotions & Stress: How to manage them (K. Chandiramani)
9. As A Man Thinketh & The Eight Pillars of Prosperity (James Allen)
10. The Science of Getting Rich (Wallace D. Wattles)
11. Chicken Soup for the Soul: Think Positive: 101 Inspirational Stories (Jack Canfield, Mark Victor Hansen & Amy Newmark).
12. How to be Assertive in Any Situation (Hadfield S. & Hasson, G.)

13. It's Not Over Until You Win (Les Brown)
14. Dare to Win (Jack Canfield and Mark Victor Hansen)
15. Feel the Fear and do it anyway (Susan Jeffers)
16. Do it or Ditch it (Bev James)
17. Flourish (Martin Seligman)

My Suggested YouTube Motivational Speakers (These are just a few, you can search for more).

1. Bob Proctor
2. Tony Robbins
3. Nichola James Vujicic
4. Joel Osteen
5. Lee Brown
6. Jim Rohn
7. Brian Tracy
8. Jack Canfield
9. Positive affirmations by Jason Stephenson
10. Lisa Nichols

Author Bio

Peggy Bareh is an inspirational award-winning author, empowerment leader, independent domestic abuse advocate and CEO of I AM Thriving Now; The World's most inspirational global movement for one million abuse survivors to transform their trauma into triumph.

Having lost all hope after a lifetime of abuse, Peggy suffered terribly from zero-confidence, a paralysing fear of rejection, and debilitating depression.

Hanging onto her faith, she built up the courage to leave the abusive relationship with her partner, taking her three children to embark on a three-year journey of self-discovery that would change their lives forever.

Peggy learned how to transform her Trauma into Triumph, creating a unique recovery toolkit called 'I AM Thriving Now', which unlocks the greatness of every life that this powerful program touches.

Peggy has inspired and transformed hundreds of lives already and is now on a Global mission to empower you to thrive, not just to survive.

Printed in Great Britain
by Amazon